THE SOCIAL MOBILE MARKETING GUIDE FOR SMALL BUSINESSES

GEORGE TRAN

Copyright ©2013 Mango Tree Mobile LLC

ISBN: 1482089289

ISBN 13: 9781482089288

WARNING:
THIS BOOK MAY BE OUT OF DATE

Mobile marketing and social media is constantly changing. I periodically update this book as I find new strategies that work (and those that don't work).

To download a FREE up-to-date version of the book, please come to

www.socialmobilemarketingguide.com

– or –

scan this Quick Response (QR) code using your smartphone.

(Go on, try it. Bring out your smartphone, load up any "QR code reader" app from the App Store, and aim it at the square. It's fun.)

WHAT MAKES THIS
BOOK DIFFERENT?

This book is unlike any other marketing book on social media and mobile marketing. While other books tell you every conceivable way to use mobile technology and how to do it, I am going to show you just a few high-impact strategies that you can implement quickly, that do not cost a fortune, and that have been proven to work. To be clear, this is not a complete soup-to-nuts marketing book. This book is designed **to inspire you to take real, massive action to grow your business**. Too often, businesspeople read marketing books, then put them down and never do anything with their new knowledge.

When I decided to write this book, I was going to write strictly about mobile marketing because it was such a huge opportunity. However, as I reviewed the behavior of customers, as well as my own, I realized that a marketing campaign strictly based on mobile media is only half the equation. Most people with a smartphone these days use a combination of both social media and mobile media to find the businesses they choose to patronize.

This is why I called this book *The Social Mobile Marketing Guide for Small Businesses*. I will be focusing on both *social* and *mobile* marketing. I call this **SoMo Marketing**.

Rather than being a regular, boring nonfiction how-to book, this book is a story about Emily and her journey toward mastering SoMo Marketing. I want to keep the learning light and enjoyable.

Keep in mind that I am going to focus on the power and strategy of mobile marketing and make certain assumptions about its execution. In almost every case illustrated, the business owner is assumed to be working with a marketing firm or a web designer/technologist. I have deliberately left the minutia of the execution out.

"Why would you leave us hanging like that?" I hear you say. Look, it is quite simple. I want to show you a few easy techniques to **help you make more money** so you can focus on what you are good at and *not* **be a propellerhead techno geek**. My aim is to help you focus on the overall goal and the marketing strategy of your business, rather than to frustrate and confuse you with the technology and its implementation. You should let the geeks handle the complicated stuff so you can focus on growing your business.

THE FREE MANGO TREE MOBILE COACHING PROGRAM

As a companion to the book, I have also created a free coaching program to guide you through the implementation of a SoMo Marketing strategy for your own business.

The coaching program will show you how to implement many of the strategies discussed in this book. It includes videos with step-by-step instructions on how to create a coupon, SMS autoresponders, and a whole lot more.

This would cost you many thousands of dollars if you were to work with a marketing firm. As my gift to you, *I am giving this coaching program to you free of charge.* The price of admission for the program is your goodwill and word of mouth. I just ask that you tell your friends about Mango Tree Mobile.

For more information about the coaching program, visit

http://www.mangotree.mobi/coachingprogram.

Thank you for your kind and generous support.

George Tran

CONTENTS

Chapter 1

Emily's New Assignment

"Beep! Beep! Beep!" chimes Emily's iPhone.

It's 7:00 a.m., and it's time to wake up. She rolls over in bed and reaches for her iPhone to see if there are any e-mails or text messages she missed while she slept. She listens to a message from Kat. Kat is free this afternoon and wants to get together for lunch. She asks Emily to recommend something.

Using her iPhone, she quickly browses Facebook to see what her friends are up to. Since buying her iPhone, she hardly touches her computer anymore. She keeps up-to-date with what's going on in her world and her friends' lives via the Facebook and Twitter apps.

After a quick shower and breakfast, she drives through The Supreme Bean, her favorite coffee stand. While there, she sees a sign that says, "Scan your phone here and receive a free coffee after ten purchases." Since she frequents Supreme Bean, she whips out her iPhone and scans it against the QR code affixed to the side of the coffee hut.

"There you go," says the blond teenager as he hands her the latte. "You wouldn't believe how many people try to game the system. They will come by and just scan the board a few times in an effort to get multiple credits per visit. Thank goodness the system is set up automatically so that you only get one credit per visit, or we would have gone out of business." They share a good chuckle, and Emily drives off to work.

She is quite nervous because today Maria wants to see her for a special assignment. Maria is the owner of the three-restaurant chain where Emily works. Emily is the assistant manager at one of the restaurants and has no idea why the meeting was called. Maria wants Emily to report to the office at Gino's Pizza first thing in the morning. Steeling herself, Emily approaches Maria's office.

"Good morning, Emily," Maria says as Emily knocks on the door of her office. Maria's office looks like the Tasmanian Devil had a field day in it. It's amazing anyone can even work in that environment. In fact, Emily has offered to help her tidy her office, but Maria insists that she has a system. Despite all appearances, Maria seems to know where almost everything is.

"You're probably wondering why I have asked you in this morning," said Maria as she cleared a chair for Emily. "I like you, Emily. I think you will go far with us. You are diligent, young, and full of ideas. You are not like some of my managers, who stick to doing things just because that's what we've always done. You see, my family has been in the pizza business since 1984, and things have changed a lot since then. We've done pretty well, as you can see, and we've got three restaurants in Chicago now. However, I feel that we're stagnating, particularly in the area of marketing.

"I have been paying for a *Yellow Pages* ad for as long as I can remember, and frankly, I don't know if people even use it these days. To be honest with you, I don't even remember the last time I actually opened up a *Yellow Pages*. I've also been paying for ads with coupon companies to promote Gino's, yet I want to see if I can do better.

"I want to take this restaurant to a higher level and improve upon what my father left when he passed away. I see all these new changes happening around me, such as social media and mobile technology, and I have no idea how to use them to grow my business. All I know about mobile phones is that I have one and I use it to check my e-mail.

"This is where you come in. I want you to spend the next couple of weeks researching everything you can about this and come back to me with a proposal about what we can do to grow our business. I've given Susie a temporary promotion to take over your position while you are working on this project for me.

"To help you get started, I will introduce you to a few of my friends who are using Facebook and mobile marketing for their businesses. I would have loved to do it myself but, as you can see," Maria says, gesturing toward the piles of paperwork on her desk, "I'm just too busy." She slides a sheet of paper toward Emily with the names and phone numbers of a few people.

"And by the way, Emily, the idea is to save money. Don't get any fancy ideas. Times are tough, and we're looking for ways to grow our business but not completely overhaul our business. I am looking for quick, simple things I can implement quickly and affordably."

As Maria finishes her sentence, her phone rings, so she waves Emily out of the office.

CHAPTER 2

THE OPPORTUNITY

Emily is stunned. How is she going to do this? She knows nothing of mobile marketing or social media. Sure, she has an iPhone and uses Facebook, but so what? Just then, she remembers that she has a lunch date with Kat. Kat is somewhat of a technology guru. Emily often relies on Kat for advice about technology and what things to buy. Kat is a web designer and Internet marketer, and Emily can spend their lunch together picking her brain. She brings out her iPhone and searches for the nearest Mexican restaurant. She knows that Kat loves Mexican food, and a plate of nachos might be just the thing to open the conversation.

Emily opens Google Maps and searches for "Mexican restaurants." She then uses the global positioning system (GPS) on her phone to locate all the Mexican restaurants in the area. She notices that some have reviews and some don't. She scans only the ones with reviews. When she finds one that looks interesting, she clicks on the restaurant's website to check out the menu and prices. This website is not mobile-friendly. It's big, fancy, and slow to load. It is hard for her to navigate because the site is designed for a larger desktop screen.

Frustrated, she closes the desktop site and picks Taco Loco, the next one with good reviews on the list. This site is designed with a mobile user in mind. It shows the restaurant's address, pictures of the restaurant, and its menu with prices. It has easy links on the site to more of the restaurant's reviews on Yelp.com and an easy map location button, which will show her exactly how to get to the restaurant from where she is currently.

She sends Kat a text message to meet her at Taco Loco and includes the link. She grabs a notebook and a pen and heads to the restaurant. Emily has a lot to think about and figures that she might have better luck organizing her thoughts somewhere outside of her office. Fortunately, her phone guides her through the streets of Chicago right to the restaurant, as her mind is already swirling with her new assignment.

When Emily arrives at Taco Loco, she is seated at a nice corner booth. She is given a menu and notices that it has a QR code in the front. It says, "Please check in on Facebook. Just scan the QR code below. We give away $50 every week to people who check in on our Facebook page." She figures she might as well try it so she can start learning what others are doing with mobile media.

Emily scans the QR code with her iPhone and is directed to Taco Loco's website. On the mobile-friendly site, there is a quick link to Taco Loco's Facebook check-in and Facebook "like" buttons. She clicks on both of these buttons.

Emily also notices that there is a sign on the table that says, "Join our VIP club. Just send a text message to 55555 with the words 'freedrink' to be notified of regular specials and discounts. When you join our club, as a special welcome, you will receive any non-alcoholic drink on the house."

Soon after sending the SMS, she receives her free drink from her waitress. All she had to do was show the waitress the message she received on her cell phone.

Emily opens her notebook and stares at the page. She knows this lunch with Kat will help her get started on her new assignment. She begins to make a list of interview questions.

Just before noon, Kat strolls in, scoots into the booth next to Emily, gives her a hug, immediately scans the QR code, and checks into Taco Loco on Facebook. Kat says to Emily, "Long time, no speak. How are things?"

"Generally, great! I've settled into the new neighborhood pretty well, though I still need to find a vet for Jacks. Been busy with work. The boss gave me a new assignment that has my brain spinning. She wants me to learn all about mobile marketing and come up with a recommendation. Unfortunately, besides owning an iPhone, I know very little about the subject.

"I see a lot of companies starting to implement mobile media and social media strategies, like this restaurant, for example. Unfortunately, it all seems like rocket science, and I don't fancy sitting down and reading for two weeks solid. As luck would have it, you're here. Maybe you can give me a quick introduction about this stuff. Besides, their reviews say they have a mean plate of nachos here, and they're on me if you can shed some light."

Kat laughs. "That's too funny. My company has been growing like crazy. We started as a web design company and began moving into mobile and social marketing as the trends pulled us in that direction. Our clients started retaining us to help them with their online marketing, and now more and more clients are asking us to help them with a mobile marketing strategy too.

"My expertise is not really in mobile marketing. I know the basics. My partner, Mark, is the guy you'll want to talk to about that.

I'll be happy to tell you what I know, since you're buying the nachos. Call that my consulting fee."

"You're on! I'll even spring for the extra guacamole."

"An offer I can't refuse! It's like you know me," Kat chuckles. "At the risk of missing any of the important basics, I'm going to assume you're starting at ground zero."

"You might even say I'm starting somewhere in the subbasement," Emily sighs.

"That's OK," soothes Kat. "I've got the key to the elevator. The first thing you've got to understand is that we're at the beginning of a huge revolution. Nothing like this has happened since the advent of the Internet. Let me ask you, when was the last time you checked your e-mail on your desktop?"

"About two weeks ago, when I was doing some research on my computer. Other than that, I do all my personal e-mail from my iPhone."

"Exactly! That's my point. You don't see people walking around with their laptop too often and certainly don't see people strolling down the sidewalk with their desktops and monitors laid out on a cart before them. Even though we use desktop computers at work, fewer and fewer people are running home to sit in front of yet another monitor—except for us online gamers, that is. When I'm gaming, yes, I want my big computer and monitor, yet I rarely use it for shopping or e-mail. For that, I pull out my mobile wherever I happen to be. Almost everyone has a cell phone these days, and according the latest research from Google, over a hundred and ten million people in the United States alone have smartphones. People are constantly fondling their smartphones. You know, you check your e-mails, play games, and use Facebook with your friends all the time."

Emily responds fervently, "But those pigs must die for what they did! They had it coming for stealing the eggs of those poor birds!"[1]

They both laugh.

Kat continues, "So, you clearly are part of the mobile revolution, but do you know how big the revolution is? Hang on to your seat—Google says it expects mobile searches to exceed desktop usage by as soon as two thousand fourteen. In fact, it has said that its mobile business will dwarf its desktop business. Can you see why this is such a big deal?"

Emily is speechless; she had not realized the change was so dramatic.

"I mean, seriously, Em, take a look around. Nearly everyone has access to SMS. I don't even call people anymore; I just send people a message and know that within five minutes or so, I'll get a response back.[2]

"My clients constantly tell me the reason why they are using mobile marketing is because it is more responsive. Unlike radio, newspaper ads, or—worse still—TV ads, it is very hard to track ROI [return on investment]. You'd throw money at a wall and pray that, hopefully, someone would listen. With mobile marketing, my clients can tell right away whether their ads are working or not through the number of responses they receive.

"Look, if most of your customers are no longer paying attention to TV, radio, or newspaper ads, then why would you want to advertise there? Why not put yourself in front of a device they constantly have with them?"

---

1   This is a reference to Angry Birds, a popular mobile game.

2   According to Google, over 97 percent% of text messages are read within five minutes of being sent. See (Google, "The Mobile Movement: Understanding Smartphone Users,", April 2011.)

Their conversation is interrupted when a man approaches the table and asks, "Are you trying to recruit Emily to join our company?"

Both Emily and Kat are surprised to see Mark. "Mark! What are you doing here?" asks Emily with a smile.

"I hope I am not interrupting anything. I was just around the corner finishing up with a client and was getting ready to head to lunch when I saw your check-in post on Facebook, so I decided to pop over. Is it OK to join you? They have killer nachos here."

"Wonderful!" exclaims Kat. "Sit down. The nachos are on Emily, and you can help explain mobile marketing to her. Her boss has tasked her with the job of figuring out a mobile marketing strategy for her company."

Mark's face breaks into a grin. "That's awesome, Emily. You know, Kat and I can just come in and do it all for you. We're pretty good at this sort of stuff."

"I know, Mark," says Emily. "My boss specifically wants me to go out and learn this stuff myself and lead the change internally. No offense, but you guys are not cheap. However, once I figure all these things out, I am sure we will need your help to put it all together. I am not a geek and have no interest in getting bogged down with the execution. I want to understand the technology, put together a strategy that management will approve, and then work with someone to help make it happen."

Mark nods and says, "That's smart. I wish more companies took this approach instead of trying to do it on their own. They think they can save a few bucks learning and doing it all themselves. Unfortunately, there's just so much to learn, and if you don't know what you're doing, it can actually blow up in your face."

"So, Mark, you want to take over?" asks Kat.

"Would love to." Mark settles into the booth. "One of the things we quickly realized when we started helping our clients with their mobile marketing strategies is that mobile marketing and social media are intimately tied together. Take this meeting as an example. Because you ladies checked into Facebook, I was able to come join you. In fact, Miguel, the owner of Taco Loco, is one of our clients. We helped set him up with many of the things he is using for his business.

"People no longer trust companies. Instead, people have come to rely more and more on the opinions of their friends and peer reviews. This is why places like Amazon, Yelp, Foursquare, and Google are doing so well. These are places in which people can write reviews and give feedback and ratings about restaurants and other businesses.

"Let me give you an example. When you were deciding which phone to get, did you rely on a newspaper or TV ad?"

"No," Emily replies. "Actually, I remember the whole thing. I had dropped my phone and needed to get a new one. I actually went on Facebook and asked my friends about what they recommended for a new phone. A few of them recommended an Android phone because it was more flexible, and some recommended Apple. I couldn't decide until I consulted with Kat. She had an iPhone and recommended it, so that's what I got."

Mark nods and smiles. "So you didn't see an ad on TV and say to yourself, 'I've got to get myself an iPhone'?"

"Nope," responds Emily.

"That's what I am talking about. That's the power of social media," says Mark. "When social media is combined with mobile marketing, it produces an incredible synergy. We call it **SoMo Marketing**, our shortcut for Social Mobile Marketing.

"Social media allows you to tap into this phenomenon called viral marketing. If your business or product 'goes viral,' it is spread from one person to another like a virus. If you have a proper incentive and mechanism to do so, it can work incredibly well.

"Before we go too deeply into this, perhaps I can give you an introduction to the basics of mobile marketing."

"Sounds great! I'm all ears."

CHAPTER 3

EMILY LEARNS MOBILE MARKETING BASICS

"I am going to presume you know what an SMS message is," Mark begins.

Emily nods. "Of course. I send texts every day. I know it can only be a hundred and sixty characters long, at most. When I send a message to a friend, it costs me money, and when my friend receives it, it also costs her money."

"There's a difference between SMS when it is used by an individual compared to SMS when it is used by a company," Mark clarifies. "Most people have unlimited SMS phone plans these days. This means that you can send as many as you want and receive as many as you want.

"However, for a company to use SMS for commercial purposes, it will need to purchase some sort of commercial SMS plan from a service provider. Typically, the company pays a monthly fee starting at fifty dollars per month and up. This entitles the company to a certain number of credits that can be used to send SMS messages to people.

"One thing I really want to make sure you understand is how effective SMS is. As a marketer, I know that people are getting more and more resistant to marketing messages. They no longer pay attention to ads like they used to. When we send out e-mail broadcasts, we don't get many responses because spam filters target mass e-mail campaigns and people just aren't paying attention to e-mail as much. However, what makes me very excited about SMS is that, according to studies done by Google, about ninety-seven percent of SMS messages are read within five minutes of being sent."

Emily is impressed. "Wow, that's effective for marketing. So how does a business acquire a list of people? Is that what happens when I join Taco Loco's VIP club?"

Mark grins wickedly. "You're catching on, Emily. That's what we call **list acquisition activity**. We come up with an incentive program to give people a reason to opt in to a business's mailing list. As you mentioned earlier, it costs the business money to send out a message and it costs the recipient money to receive it. As such, we have to give more consideration to what we send out. More is not better. We will talk about that later.

"Next, let's talk about a **short code**. In order to opt in to Taco Loco's VIP club, you sent a message to five-five-five-five-five. Well, that's what's known as a short code. It is a universal number that is nationally recognized. It is essentially Taco Loco's marketing 'phone number,' but it's only five digits long. The phone companies did this so it is a lot easier to remember than a standard phone number. Most of the time, this short code is shared among many other business owners."

Surprised, Emily exclaims, "Wait a minute! If other people are using the same number, how would the people who join our mailing list be earmarked for my company?"

Mark smiles and explains, "That's where the keyword 'freedrink' comes in. In other words, anyone who sends a text message to five-five-five-five-five with the keyword 'freedrink' will be earmarked as someone belonging to Taco Loco's SMS mailing list. Taco Loco could have quite a few keywords, depending on how sophisticated its marketing campaign is and what sort of marketing plan it subscribes to, but every one of those keywords is unique to that numeric short code. While 'freedrink' texted to five-five-five-five-five belongs to Taco Loco, typing 'freedrink' and texting it to five-five-five-five-six may opt you into a different business's list."

"So let me get this straight," Emily says. "If I sign up with you guys, I will likely get the same short code. However, I could have a keyword of say 'freesidedish' as well as another one called 'pizzavip' depending on my campaign. Both of these keywords belong to me, and anyone who sends a text message to five-five-five-five-five with either keyword will be opted into my list?"

Mark nods. "That's correct."

"And whenever I want to send out an announcement, like when we have a slow day, I could send a special offer to either list—or both lists—if I want to. Depending on the size of the list, I will be charged for every recipient on my broadcast. Is that right?" Emily asks.

"You are correct again," Mark says. "Most plans allot a credit per SMS and sell those allotments in packages to match the size of the opt-in list.

"While it is seldom used, there's another type of code called a **long code**. A long code is exactly like a short code but looks like a regular phone number. Long codes are easier to buy and are much more readily available. Of course, the downside is that it is longer and harder for people to remember."

Mark pauses for a moment to sip his drink while Emily absorbs what he has told her. "Now I'll introduce you to **QR codes**. I love QR codes.

"A QR code is one of those square bar code things you see on menus, posters, advertisements, and websites. It allows marketers to make it easy and convenient for customers to connect to businesses simply by scanning the code with their smartphones or tablets. The QR code can be programmed to lead the customer to the business's main website or a specific offer page and can even prepare an SMS to a short code with the keyword all ready so that all the customer has to do is hit the send button. It's incredibly powerful yet also flexible."

Emily furrows her brows a moment. "I know this may sound too obvious to you, but Kat was the one who set up my phone for me. Where do I find a QR code scanner? I need to be able to explain this to Maria."

"It's simple. Just go to the app store on your smartphone and search for 'QR code reader.' You will see a bunch of them. Most are free, and any one of them will do. Just install it and run the app. It will turn on your rear-facing camera, which you point at the QR code, and it will then read it and do the appropriate action, as specified by the QR code.

"The beauty with QR codes is that they make it much easier for customers to connect with a business. Whether it's to join a promotional list or add their contact information into the phone, it's super simple for businesses to keep themselves in front of their customers.

"A QR code is great because it makes it easy for your customers to do business with you whenever you need them to act as a result of your ads. We call this a 'call to action.'

"A call to action is what we want our customers to do at the end of our marketing activity. Whether we place an ad in the newspaper, make a radio ad, or create a display sign at the cash register, the call to action is the step we want the customer to take. It may be to pick up the phone and call a number or to fill in e-mail information to receive a special offer.

"Sadly, many businesses often do not have a call to action for their ads. You'd be amazed how often that happens. If you don't tell people what to do, they end up not doing anything. It's that simple."

Emily smiles. "Hmm. I guess that's one of the things I will be fixing when I get back to the office. Our newspaper ad doesn't really have a call to action. When I was learning about this stuff, my marketing professor said it was called 'branding.' The idea is that you just place your ad in front of people and hope that if they see it enough times, they may eventually act."

Mark laughs. "So how's that working for you?"

Sheepishly, Emily responds, "I don't know, to be honest. I don't think even Maria, my boss, knows. It's one of those cases where that's the way it's always been done. This is why she's having me do this research. There's no accountability for what we've been doing."

"Yep," Mark says, nodding. "We see that all the time. Companies are so fixed in their way of doing business that they don't even realize they are throwing money down the toilet month after month."

Mark reaches for the menu and points to Taco Loco's QR code at the top right hand-corner. "With Taco Loco, we've keyed the

QR code on the menu. When customers aim their smartphones at the code, they will be brought to the mobile version of Taco Loco's website."

Mark continues, "We can also key the **QR code with a message**. For example, if it was my business card, I could have my name, phone number, e-mail address, address, and hours of operation on the QR code. When customers scan my QR code on my business card, they will have all my contact information swiped onto their phone. This will save them from having to type my information into their address book. They can then copy and paste that information into their address book. The idea is to make it simpler for my customers to do business with me.

This is a QR code encoded with a "www" address.

If you have never seen a QR code at work, please have your smartphone or tablet out and search for any app under the words "QR Code Reader."

Once your QR code reader app is installed, launch it. Your front-facing camera should activate. Simply aim the camera at each of the codes in this book and see what happens. This is a great way to gain first-hand experience as to what each QR code can do for your business.

"Another thing we can do with a **QR code is to encode it to call a phone number**. For example, if Gino's Pizza had a QR code on its pizza boxes with a phone number action, every time customers scanned the QR code with their phones, their phones would automatically ring your incoming order line.

"You can also encode a **QR code to send an SMS**. This feature will make it easier for customers to opt in to my list. As you recall, to opt in to a list, customers will need to send an SMS message to a specific short code with a specially assigned keyword.

This is what a QR code with a message looks like.

Instead of asking them to type out the actual phone number and then the message, we can just encode the QR code to send the message for our opt-in short code plus our keyword.

"And finally, you can encode a **QR code to send an e-mail**. This is very similar to sending an SMS, except this opens up the e-mail application with your pre-designated e-mail address. For example, let's say you run an ad in a magazine and your call to action is to have the customers send an e-mail to sales for more informa-

tion. You might want to include a QR code to send an e-mail to sales@ yourcompany.com. This way, when they scan the QR code, their devices will open up the e-mail application with your e-mail address already populated in the 'To' field."

This is a QR code with a phone number.

Mark sits back in his chair. "OK, that wraps it up for our basic understanding of some of the fundamental concepts of mobile marketing."

"Thank you so much, Mark. That was incredibly helpful, and these nachos are incredibly delicious, so what do you say to a second order?"

After they place the order, Mark asks Emily if she will write a review of Taco Loco for Miguel, the owner of the restaurant. Emily responds, "Sure. How? And why would I do that?"

Mark smiles. "I'm glad you asked."

This is a QR code with an SMS message.

This is a QR code that sends an e-mail

CHAPTER 4

EMILY LEARNS THE POWER OF SOCIAL MEDIA

"That is a great question." Kat says. "This is the first time you've been here, right? How did you choose Taco Loco?"

"Well, I did a search for Mexican restaurants. The first one on the list didn't have any reviews, and the website was too hard to read on my phone. The second one was Taco Loco. I liked it because a lot of people gave it very good reviews and the website was mobile friendly. It loaded fast and had easy links to Yelp. After reviewing what other people said on Yelp, I decided to give Taco Loco a try. Several of the people specifically mentioned the nachos, and I know you love that dish."

With a devilish grin, Mark asks Emily, "Do you think that that was an accident? Or do you think perhaps we had something to do with that?"

Emily's mouth drops. "Oh my goodness! I've been using social media and not even realizing it. So what you are saying is that you've worked with Miguel to have people in the restaurant post reviews on Google and other social media properties? And by asking me to write a review for Taco Loco, I am helping other people choose Taco Loco in favor of other Mexican restaurants in the area?"

"I am the social media person for the company," Kat says. "When Miguel first came to us, we helped him plan his SoMo Marketing. We advised him to trade inexpensive items for reviews on social media websites. He used to offer free drinks or free soups if his customers would write a review on one of these social media properties. Essentially, he paid them in soups and sodas to take the time to write their opinions. This serves two purposes: it leaves feedback for the restaurant, which builds credibility, and if it was negative feedback, it allows him the opportunity to fix it."

"You mean he was bribing them?" Emily asks.

"Absolutely not!" says Kat. "One of the things we were very adamant about when we were coaching Miguel was that social media values authenticity above all else. He was very clear about this when he asked people to write reviews for him. He would tell them that the gift was just his way of thanking his customers for taking the time out of their busy day to write a review for him. They were not obliged in any way to give him a positive review. And invariably, some people didn't give very good reviews. However, what won people over was that Miguel would go to these sites and read each comment himself. If there was a valid complaint, he was able to respond to that customer and take steps to fix the problem. He was never defensive and did not get into an argument with his customers. He used the comments as constructive criticism, and that made people love him more."

"Wow, that's pretty brave," Emily says admiringly. "Our restaurant gets all sorts. Sometimes they just have a bad day and decide to misbehave. I am not sure if Maria would approve of such open dialogue."

"Well, that's the risk you take if you want to play the social media game," Kat says. "If you try to fake it and get caught, there's usually a huge backlash. Your online credibility will be shot.

"The advantage of using social media is that more and more often, people are coming to depend upon the opinions of other consumers. We call this 'crowd sourcing.' These social media properties have several advantages. Because so many people use them, they are highly ranked on search engines. If your restaurant is discussed on a popular social media site, chances are a huge demographic will read that discussion. People who never heard of you before will see you for the first time. You have three restaurants in Chicago to cover a wider geographic population of customers. Locals come to know you and become regulars. With social media sites, even people passing through Chicago looking for pizza will find you. Now that's a customer you truly wouldn't have had otherwise. Basically, when you engage in a real social media campaign and do it right, you will attract more customers without really trying."

"So this is sort of like a gigantic word-of-mouth pool of people?" asks Emily.

"Exactly," responds Kat. "On Taco Loco's site, we made sure to put links to all the relevant social media properties such as Yelp, Facebook and Google Plus for Taco Loco. This way it will be easy for his customers to go to various social media properties right off his **mobile website**."

"I notice you said 'his mobile website.' Does that mean he has two websites—one for his desktop visitors and one for his mobile visitors?"

"Correct," says Kat. "Miguel originally hired us to design his regular desktop website. That's how we got started. When he came to us for help with his mobile campaign, we told him he needed a mobile website, as the needs of a mobile user are very different from those of a regular desktop user.

"Desktop users typically are at their desks. They have more bandwidth and a bigger screen, so we can show a lot more things on a desktop website. A mobile user is usually browsing from a tablet or a smartphone, like an iPhone. As you've experienced before, it is sometimes challenging to view a desktop website on a mobile device.

"Besides, mobile users are looking for very different things than desktop users are. They typically have less bandwidth and are on the road. They need very specific quick things from your mobile site.

"When we designed Taco Loco's original site, Miguel wanted to have some Spanish background music playing for his visitors, as well as a video. We decided the best way to do that was to use this technology called Flash from Adobe. Unfortunately, while that may work well on the desktop, it was a disaster on an iPhone. Steve Jobs decided that iPhones did not need Flash and made an executive decree that iPhones would never support Flash. This means that people coming to Taco Loco's desktop website on their iPhone or iPad would see a blank page. So when we found out that Miguel wanted to engage in a mobile campaign, we knew we needed to design him a separate mobile website."

"So what is the difference between a mobile website and a desktop website, besides the obvious?" asks Emily.

"One thing to keep in mind," Kat explains, "is that the head space of mobile users is often different than that of desktop users. They are on the go. This means they don't have a lot of time to read a long article or spend hours appreciating your site. They just need basic information and links to useful things that are relevant to them.

"For example, on Taco Loco's website, we put his address, his phone number, and his hours of operation right at the top of the screen to make it easy for people on the go to find and contact Taco Loco. We even linked the address to Google Maps so that people can just click on the address and be given directions from where they are to Taco Loco. And of course, when visitors hit his phone number, their devices will dial Taco Loco's phone number automatically. You can't do this on a regular website.

"Because we also engaged in a number of social media campaigns for Miguel, we wanted to make it easy for his customers to quickly and easily hit the different review sites, such as Yelp, Foursquare, and Zugat. This serves two purposes: it allows people who want to look at reviews for Taco Loco to easily do so, and it enables people who want to share their experiences with any of these social media properties to quickly and easily do so without having to search for it.

"We posted lots of pictures of Taco Loco to give people an idea of what the restaurant looks like and the different dishes it has and included pictures of some famous people who have frequented the restaurant. We listed the menu items to make it easy for people to see the menu on their mobile devices.

"We had a short video of Miguel greeting his visitors on his desktop website. That was also done in Flash. We had to convert that to a YouTube format so it can also play on iPhones and iPads.

"To encourage people to come to his restaurant and opt in to his VIP club, Miguel also has his mobile coupon right on his mobile site. All people have to do is hit the link to send an SMS to five-five-five-five-five with the keyword 'freedrink.'

"And finally, we put in a link to his desktop website at the bottom. Most Android devices support Flash, and we want to make it flexible so that if visitors want to see the main desktop website, they can."

Emily considers what Kat has said. "Wow, that's a lot to take in. So what you are saying is that we will need a mobile website in addition to our regular website, that the mobile website should include our contact information, which should be automatically connected to call the restaurant and link to the Google Maps program, and that if we have any coupons or opt-ins, we should make them easily linked to the SMS messenger. We need to convert all our videos to YouTube so they can be universally viewed. Then we should put links to all the relevant social media properties for our business to make it easy for our customers to see and make reviews.

"Also, we should include up to ten pictures of our business, our products, or anything else that will help get visitors to choose our business over our competitors. And we should also put a link at the bottom at the mobile site to our main site, in case people want to see the main site. Did I get that right?"

"Perfect," responds Kat. "You're a quick learner."

CHAPTER 5

EMILY LEARNS ABOUT FACEBOOK

After lunch, Kat invites Emily to return with her and continue the conversation. Mark thanks Emily for the nachos and promises to catch up with her later, as he has another appointment in the city. Emily grabs her notebook, and they walk over to Kat's office to delve more deeply into social media marketing.

"Kat, I have a basic understanding of Facebook from a user's perspective. Can you please go into more detail about the different social media properties?"

"Sure," Kat agrees. "Though before we go into social media, I want to talk about a few fundamentals. The first thing you need to understand is 'social equity.'

"Social equity is your online reputation. People like to talk. If you have great service, people want to share that with their friends. If you provide terrible customer service, people want to complain

27

to their friends. The difference between your social 'goodness' and your social 'badness' is called your social equity.

"In Taco Loco's case, the restaurant has a pretty high social equity because it has quite a few reviews on a lot of social media sites. Most of them are positive."

"In our case, I don't even know what people are saying about Gino's," Emily admits. "So if we make it harder for people to talk about us, is that a good thing or is that a case of 'what you don't know may kill your business?'"

"Look, people will talk. People want to share. If you don't make it easy for them to talk, they will find someplace to talk, and you may not know where that is. They will either brag about you or complain. The problem for you is that if it is not in a forum that is easily managed, you have no way of knowing what conversations are happening around your brand and, more importantly, how to deal with negative feedback.

"I recall this one incident where several customers complained about poor service at Taco Loco on Yelp. Miguel contacted these reviewers and asked for more information. It turns out that the waiter they had was not very good. Miguel had to get rid of him and get a new waiter. Because of the complaints, he was able to correct something that was damaging his business. He was so grateful that he actually gave the reviewers a twenty-five-dollar gift certificate to Amazon.com.

"This is how you can manage your brand online. You're showing the world that you are being proactive. In social media we make the analogy of two gladiators fighting as the world watches. There's a saying about social media I love: 'what happens on social media stays online forever.'"

"What about Facebook?" Emily asks. "I know there are a lot of tricks you can do to get additional exposure of Facebook. Can you talk a little bit about that?"

"Well, as of October two thousand and twelve, Facebook has just over one billion users on its network. Each user is sharing opinions, asking questions, and having friends openly participate in conversations. Users ask anything from 'what should I do, my daughter has this horrible rash?' to 'which smartphone I should buy?'

"As you recall my saying earlier, Em, Facebook allows users to 'check in' to almost any location to tell their friends where they are. When you check in, your activity will show up on your friend's newsfeeds. This means any friend who happens to be looking at the time will know where you are.

"Let's say, for example, that you check in to Taco Loco's every week and comment on how much you love the place. And let's say I do the same. Someone like Mark, who knows both of us, will see a Facebook entry about Taco Loco twice a week—one from you, and one from me.

"So let me ask you this: how is this any different from the branding ads you place in your newspaper for Gino's?"

Emily thinks about it and replies, "Actually, this is even more powerful than the ads because it is an endorsement coming from friends they trust. People pay attention to what their friends say, whereas people tune out ads."

"Now do you see why social media is powerful if done right? What if Gino's has one hundred of its customers check in on Facebook per day? And let's say each person has twenty friends. This gives you approximately two thousand free ad impressions per day with no cost to you.

"This is why we encourage patrons of Taco Loco to check in. In the beginning we encouraged people with things like free sides and drinks. These days people do it anyway because it has become a habit."

"That makes perfect sense. Having people check in and openly share their opinions basically constitutes free advertising and peer endorsements. So, Kat, when it comes to Facebook, I'm confused. Can you please tell me the difference between a 'like,' a check-in, and a 'share'?"

"Well, we talked about a check-in. It's just a way to tell all your friends where you currently are. You can do this by opening your Facebook app on your smartphone and hitting the check-in button on the top right corner of the screen.

"A 'like,' on the other hand, is a running total of how many people like your product, business, or offer. It's just a general vote of coolness. The more 'likes' you have, the more social equity you own. You can have a 'like' button right on your mobile-friendly website, as well as on your desktop website. When people click on the button, it shows up on their friends' newsfeeds, just like a check-in.

"A 'share' is essentially a repost. This is typically used to share movies or pictures. For example, let's say I post a really funny picture on Facebook. Because you are my friend, you see it in your newsfeed. Because it is so funny, you want to share it with your friends. You know some people I don't, so when you share it, only your friends see it. The friends we both have in common will see that both Kat and Emily have shared something.

"I highly recommend having a Facebook 'like' button on your mobile website. In order to have a 'like' button created for your mobile site, you'll need to create a Facebook fanpage."

"What's a fanpage?" Emily asks.

"Facebook is primarily designed for a person—a real, honest-to-goodness human being. This person has friends, likes, and opinions. A business, on the other hand, has no feelings or opinions. To enable business owners to differentiate their personal life from their businesses, Facebook created a fanpage concept.

"For all intents and purposes, a Facebook fanpage is exactly like a regular person. It has friends and can make posts. The difference is that a fanpage may have multiple administrators who can speak on the business's behalf.

"Instead of having friends like a regular person, Facebook fanpages have...well...fans. A person can 'like' a fanpage and become a fan of that page. With this ability, you can have your customers 'like' your fanpage and follow your business fanpage on Facebook. This way, when you want to send out an announcement, you can simply post it on your Facebook fanpage, and everyone who follows your business will receive your announcement.

"I can sit here all day and explain to you about Facebook marketing strategies, but I want us to keep focused. You can get a lot more information about Facebook marketing from other sources. There are Facebook marketing experts out there. Often people confuse the concept of free or inexpensive with simple. A Facebook marketing strategy can be free and it can be effective, but it is far from simple to manage. It can be time intensive to set up and manage if not done right. You'll have to read up on that before you decide if you want to handle Facebook on your own or hire an expert.

"Let's go to the break room and each grab a cup of tea. Then we can talk about other social media properties that might be relevant to your business, OK?"

CHAPTER 6

EMILY LEARNS ABOUT TWITTER

Emily settles back into her chair with a mug of green tea. "I have heard of **Twitter** but never used it. Can you explain what it is, why people use it, and, more importantly, how Gino's can benefit from using it?"

Kat places her tea on a coaster and responds, "Twitter is a social network that allows anyone who follows you to see your feeds, just like Facebook. Twitter has around two hundred million active people on its network, so it's no small potatoes. The big difference between Twitter and Facebook is that on Twitter, all your updates have to fit into a hundred and fourty characters because each message is—or can be—received by each of your followers via SMS.

"Gino's can use Twitter to complement its mobile marketing campaign. All you need to do is create a Twitter account and encourage your customers to follow it. Twitter also has a feature that allows users to elect to have selected Tweets sent directly to their phones through SMS. So if you follow Taco Loco and have subscribed to receive its Twitter messages as texts to your phone, you'll be updated with Taco Loco's latest information, promotions, and sales without having a Twitter app even running on your phone. What's even more amazing is that **Twitter is free to use**. It is free for the subscriber and to the business owner."

Emily narrows her eyes skeptically. "This sounds too good to be true. What's the catch?"

Kat says, "The downside of using Twitter as your SMS marketing strategy is the prerequisite that your customers sign up for Twitter. Once they sign up, you have to encourage them to have the posts sent to their phones. For many people, it's just simply too much hassle versus the reward of following you for discount offers. Plus, when I opt for Twitter to push me notifications from you, it pushes *everyone's* tweets, not just yours. If I'm paying for each text message and have dozens of Twitter accounts I'm following, that's going to be a very expensive exercise in frustration.

"Though many innovative businesses, such as coffee shops and restaurants, were quite successful at attracting followers on Twitter and were able to use Twitter as an SMS broadcast platform, I would never suggest you depend solely upon it."

Kat sips her tea, then asks Emily, "When you are looking for a new place to eat or a new service provider, what do you use?"

Emily thinks for a moment. "Well, when I first moved here, I knew nobody and didn't know where to go to eat. I used Yelp because my friend recommended it to me. Now that I think about it, I realize that I don't really pay attention to any ads in the newspapers or on TV. I didn't even go to the *Yellow Pages* to look things up; I just don't trust them."

"So what do you think about where Gino's is spending its marketing dollars?"

Emily shrugs. "I haven't really thought about it before this. Maria just pays for them as a fixed overhead expense. We don't track their effectiveness. To be honest, I don't think we would feel a difference in our business if we were to take away our *Yellow Pages* ad. I really don't remember the last time I even opened one. The funny thing is, whenever one of those huge books is delivered at my door, I think to myself, 'What a waste of paper! Someone just littered on my front steps.' I usually throw it right into the recycle bin, though one year I did use it to dry out some flowers and press them. Those big books are perfect for that. I framed them. I'll point them out the next time you come over my house."

"I'd love to see them."

"I think our newspaper ads do get some traction. People do bring in the occasional coupon we run, so there is a bit of tracking with that. The question is, are we better off spending that money on our ads or using it on our mobile media campaigns?"

Kat responds, "When we worked with Miguel, we recommended that he try moving his marketing budget from spending on ads to giving it away to his customers as free gifts instead."

"Huh? What do you mean giving it to his customers?" asks Emily.

"We came up with the idea of engaging Taco Loco's clients directly. We explained that we spend hundreds of dollars on marketing every month. To celebrate our new marketing campaign, we decided to instead give this money to our customers directly.

"We tried a couple of marketing campaigns. In the first one, we hooked up with a local nonprofit called Help the Children.[3] For every person who used a smartphone to scan Taco Loco's QR code or send an SMS to Taco Loco's opt-in number, we donated a dollar to Help the Children. We set aside a thousand dollars for

---

3   This is a fictional nonprofit for the sake of the story.

that campaign and made sure everyone understood it was not an unlimited budget.

"Anyway, we used that money within a week. The story spread quickly, as people started telling their friends about it and everyone got their friends and neighbors to opt in.

"We made a press release and invited the TV news crew to come out as we presented the check to Help the Children. This gave us even more publicity—and that was totally free publicity. What's more, we had an instant list of people we could send future offers to.

"When you think about it, acquiring a list of a thousand people at a dollar each is incredibly inexpensive."

"Agreed. And that's a nice list size, though I imagine that is dwarfed by the current list after so many social media campaigns. I must say, I'm a little envious. Then again, we all have to start somewhere." Emily pauses to jot down more notes. "You said you did two things; what was the other?"

"We gave away cash prizes to people who joined Taco Loco's opt-in list. Every week we would give away a fifty-dollar first prize and a twenty-five-dollar second prize gift certificate to Amazon. com. We wanted to show people that this is a real value exchange, not a requirement to eat at our restaurant. We made sure we took photos of the winners, pinned them on our board, and posted them online so people knew that this was legitimate. People sometimes think that these giveaways are a scam, and we wanted to prove we were truly giving the certificates to lucky winners. It was a great use of our re-budgeting efforts."

"OK, let me see if I have all this right. What I hear you say is that we should use Twitter for our mobile marketing campaign in conjunction with everything else we are doing because it is literally free. We should build a Facebook fanpage. We should reassess what we are currently spending on marketing, think creatively about how we can involve our customers in Gino's story, and reward them with prizes instead of spending it on marketing. We may want to use some sort of giveaway to a nonprofit and get the media involved to spread the good will and earn free publicity."

Kat smiles. "Why, Emily, you might make a good marketing director for Gino's yet!"

CHAPTER 7

EMILY LEARNS ABOUT YELP

Emily delves right into the next topic. "I read Yelp reviews when I was deciding what restaurant to choose for our lunch. I know Yelp is obviously a review site of some kind. What else do I need to know about it, and how can I use Yelp to help grow our restaurant business?"

"You're in the ballpark. Yelp is more than a restaurant review site; it's a total city guide. If there is a brick-and-mortar building that is open for business, it can be reviewed. I use Yelp to find restaurants, coffee kiosks, the best shops, museums—I've even used it to find the best dog parks. I know, they aren't a business, right? Still, they are a reviewable place to be, so they are listed on Yelp. It's really amazing. And what's more, Yelp will use your phone's GPS to show only the establishments in a certain radius around you. I don't care about a dog park that is several miles from my house. By the time I walk Max there, we won't need the park." Kat and Emily both grin.

"As to how you might use Yelp to help Gino's, I would equate it to a *Yellow Pages* listing. Having a presence on Yelp puts your name in the book. Being well ranked and well reviewed is like having a free ad in the book. You mentioned before, Emily, that people don't pay as much attention to ads, nor do they trust what advertisers have to say. Advertisers have to shout louder and louder these days to be heard. The problem is, the louder they shout, the more people tune them out or use ad-blocking devices like the Tivo.

"As a result, more and more people rely on the recommendations of other people in social media. Yelp has emerged as one of the premier platforms for user reviews and recommendations. What makes Yelp particularly useful for a mobile user is its ability to use location-specific data to bring up search results that provide a slew of user reviews about the business.

"Because Yelp is location specific, it's incredibly powerful. If you were driving through a city you'd never been to before and wanted to find a place to eat, you could type 'Italian restaurants' into Yelp, and it would immediately bring up a list of Italian restaurants within ten miles or so of your current location. What's more, it will also list people's feedback and ratings of the establishment. So without knowing anyone in that city, you have a very credible idea of where to eat wherever you are.

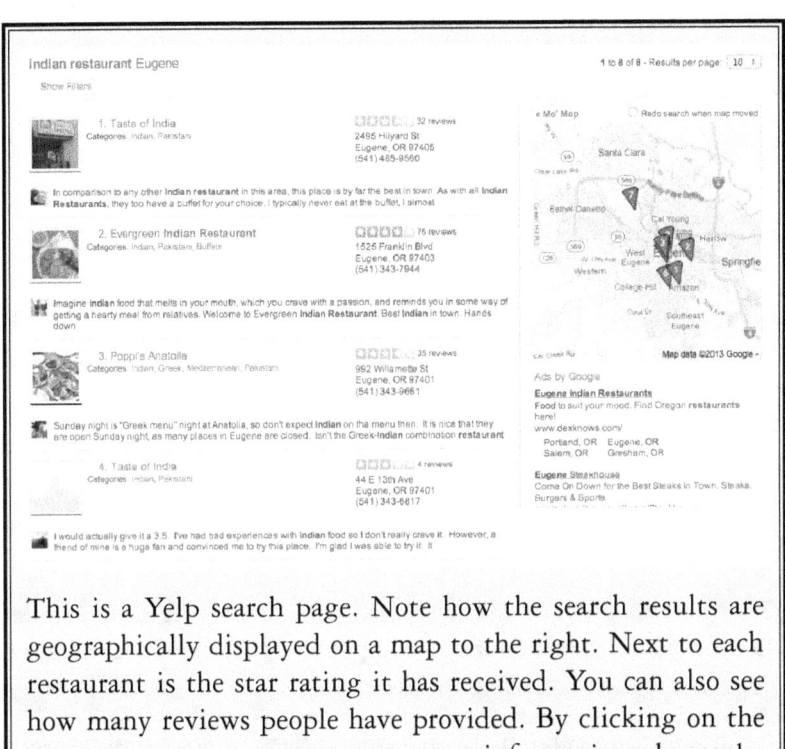

This is a Yelp search page. Note how the search results are geographically displayed on a map to the right. Next to each restaurant is the star rating it has received. You can also see how many reviews people have provided. By clicking on the restaurant name, you can see more information about the establishment.

"For diners, it is incredibly useful to be able to see the locations of the nearest restaurant as well as the ratings given by fellow users on the Yelp network. When you click on a restaurant name, you'll see a more detailed page with pictures other users have previously uploaded, reviews, maps, a link to the main website, and possibly a menu.

"As a business owner, if you don't have a Yelp entry, then you are missing out on potential free referrals. You might already have a Yelp entry without knowing it—it is either empty or has been created by one of your users. In fact, your users might already be talking about you on Yelp, for better or worse. If you create your own Yelp entry, you can customize it with accurate hours, contact information, and your own pictures. Plus, you'll be able to see what people are saying about you and have a conversation with them.

"Yelp was developed around restaurants but has since expanded to almost any category of business. You can even use it to find a tradesperson, like a plumber or an electrician.

"One way to use Yelp to grow your business is to make sure your business is registered with Yelp. Next, find out what people are saying about you. If there are negative reviews, see if they are legitimate and if you can positively address them."

Emily underlines Yelp twice in her notebook. "This looks like a pretty high-priority task for me to handle when I get back to the office. I will have to see what others have to say about Gino's on Yelp. How do you recommend we get more reviews?"

"Remember what Mark said at the restaurant, Em. Miguel offered free sodas and soups to compensate customers for the time spent giving a review. Be creative.

"Also, make sure all this is integrated with your mobile website. Make it easy for people to get to your Yelp listing so they can read your reviews as well as write their own feedback.

"Since a good portion of your traffic will be from mobile devices, you'll want to drive the Yelp reviews to a mobile-friendly website as well as to your desktop version. If you want to get your website converted to a mobile-friendly version affordably and quickly, I recommend going to www.mangotreemobile.com. The company can get your website up and ready within seven days. The best part is that you don't even have to lift a finger. The staff will do everything for you and will integrate all your social media plug-ins for you so that if people view your site from their desktop, they'll be brought to your desktop version, and if they come from a mobile device, they will automatically be brought to the mobile-friendly version. Cool, right?"

CHAPTER 8

EMILY LEARNS ABOUT FOURSQUARE

"Can you tell me more about Foursquare?" asks Emily.

"Foursquare is similar to Yelp in many ways. It, too, is a location-based site for mobile users. You can use it to check in, like one might do on Facebook, or to research businesses in an area, like you can do on Yelp. There are rankings and ratings, just like on Yelp, as well as a map. It's another site I strongly suggest you build a presence on for your business and monitor all the comments regularly."

"Hmm," Emily sighs. "The more you go into social media, the more my mind is glazing over. I kind of get it, but it also seems like it's very confusing and a lot of work."

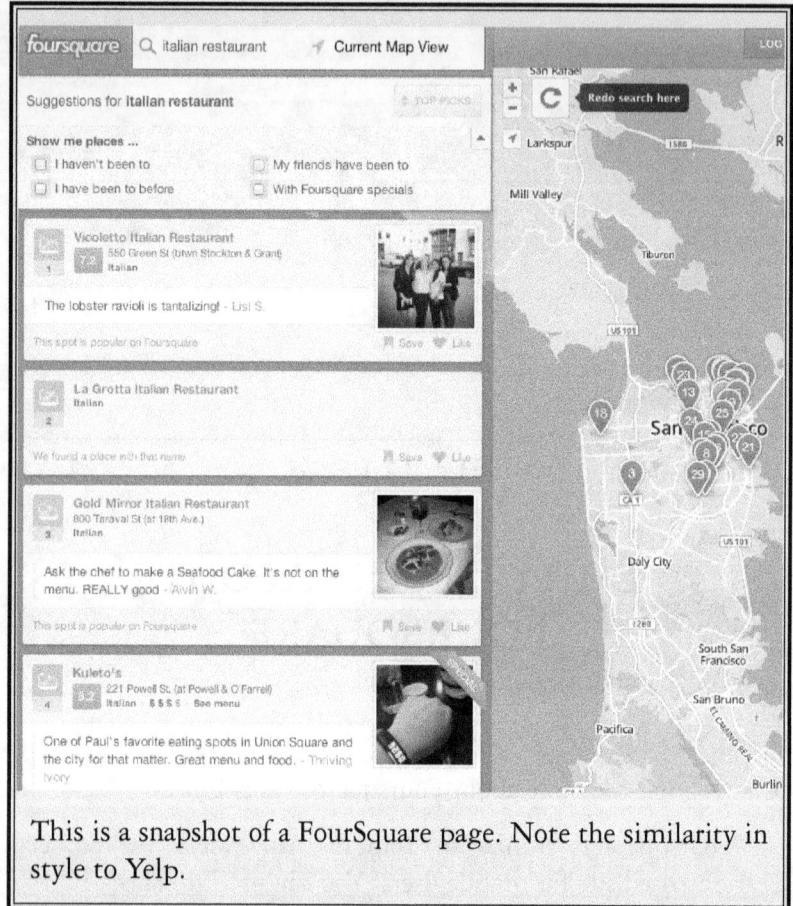

This is a snapshot of a FourSquare page. Note the similarity in style to Yelp.

Kat nods. "I couldn't agree with you more. Social media can be a huge waste of time and money if you don't know what you are doing. While it's great to understand the fundamentals of SoMo Marketing, it's often very beneficial to hire experts to do the heavy lifting for you. This is why companies hire Mark and me. We bring together the social media expertise and combine it with the mobile media piece to form a synergistic and holistic marketing strategy that is hassle free for a business owner. The reason why our business is growing is because our solution offers a better return on investment compared to what companies have been doing traditionally.

"For companies that do not have an existing social media presence, it might be easier to go to a company like Mango Tree Mobile, which specializes in helping small businesses. The company offers a package called **Mango Social** that involves the staff putting up your basic social media presence for you. For example, the company will set up your Facebook fanpage, Yelp, Foursquare, Google Maps, and a few other social media presences for just a small fixed price.

"Once these social media presences are created and established, your company can then start encouraging your clients to write feedback and reviews on them and thus begin attracting more clients through word of mouth.

"What's nice about Mango Tree Mobile is that it not only sets up your social media presence, it also creates your mobile-friendly website so that it integrates all these social media plug-ins together."

Emily asks, "Kat, I'm confused. Isn't Mango Tree Mobile a competitor to you? Why would you recommend that I go there instead of doing it myself or using you guys?"

Kat answers, "I don't recommend that you try to tackle this yourself. You guys are in the restaurant business. You know your business well, but social media and mobile marketing are not in your core competence. It makes very little sense to waste hundreds of hours learning this stuff and getting frustrated just to save yourself a few bucks.

"And while we can set all these things up for you, we're not cheap. To hire us to handle all these things would set you back thousands of dollars. Because Mango Tree Mobile specializes in this stuff, it can do the work more quickly and less expensively than we can.

"Where we shine and excel is in custom consulting. Once you have a mobile website and your social media presence established, we can help you with putting all the other pieces of your overall marketing strategy together. We can hold your hand or do it for you. That's where we earn our keep. We believe in adding value where it makes sense and showing our clients where they can get the most bang for their marketing dollar."

CHAPTER 9

EMILY LEARNS ABOUT GOOGLE MAPS

"Kat, when I go to my **Google Maps App** on my iPhone and type in 'Italian restaurants,' some restaurants show up, and some don't. Some even have reviews. I know I use this regularly and am influenced by the ratings and reviews. How does one show up on Google Maps?"

Kat fills her tea mug with water and offers to do the same for Emily as she explains, "Google is somewhat of a latecomer to the social media scene. It's making really good inroads and is quickly gaining traction. Your business should definitely be on Google Maps and get reviews as quickly as possible. More and more people are coming to rely exclusively on Google Maps on their phones for their searches and, ultimately, for their local recommendations and buying decisions.

This is a screenshot of Google Maps. It's still the same basic setup with the map and reviews.

"Many users will simply go to the Google Maps program on their iPhone or Android and search for 'Italian restaurant,' as the site will bring up something that essentially looks very similar to Yelp and Foursquare.

"To list Gino's onto Google Maps, you should go to www. google.com/places.

"Be sure to fill it out as completely as you can. You should have a Google account set up already. If you don't have a Google account, I recommend you go to www.gmail.com and set up a Gmail account.

"Alternatively, if you decide you want to use Mango Tree Mobile to do the heavy lifting for you, you can just have the consultants there set it up for you.

"On a related note, I would like to tell you about Google Plus. It's Google's version of Facebook and Twitter. While it is slow to take off, it is also something worth paying attention to.

"With Google Plus, you can post regular updates just like you do with Facebook and Twitter. What's cool about Google Plus is that it also integrates with Gmail if you are a Google mail user. This means all your e-mail contacts are automatically linked into your updates and circle of friends.

"And because it is part of Google, any 'pluses' your friends give you via Google Plus add to your coolness value on Google. Google pluses 'add up' to a greater coolness factor—and I'm not at all sorry for the pun. Through the mechanism of coolness pluses, your chances of showing up on a Google search may be increased. It's not the only thing Google looks at, but it certainly helps.

"Also, you can link your Google Maps entry to your Google Plus account. If this process is combined with lots of positive reviews, you can see how this will snowball synergistically to help bring more free word-of-mouth traffic to your site."

Emily accepts the mug of water. "Wow, I can see how Google is using its influence on the search engine side to boost the importance and applicability of Google Plus. Is this also part of Mango Social?"

"Yes, it is. The company has really thought this thing through. For many people, putting all these pieces together can be quite a project, especially if they are nontechnical and don't have a lot of time."

CHAPTER 10

EMILY LEARNS ABOUT LINKEDIN AND YOUTUBE

"What about LinkedIn?" asks Emily.

"LinkedIn.com is a professional social network. It's a different beast, yet if your business caters more to a professional customer base, then this might be a network that benefits your business.

"LinkedIn is a social networking site for professionals—the individual people, not the businesses themselves. It is meant to connect people to new people through people they already know. Do you remember the 'six degrees of separation' theory that everyone is connected to everyone by six or less degrees? Well, this is a site meant to connect you to everyone else in that way. When I uploaded my profile and résumé, I also uploaded my personal connections—all my nearest friends and acquaintances. Through LinkedIn, I was able to connect to so many other people that by the third degree, I was able to find Mark and start this business. Cool, right? It really is a small world after all, and especially with social media, we are all part of a much larger circle. LinkedIn was created to enable business owners to use their own network to potentially connect with the person they need to meet.

"Let's say you are selling some specialized medical product and you need to connect to the chief purchasing officer at a local hospital. You might want to connect to her via LinkedIn first. It's a great way to introduce yourself and to build rapport with her before trying to hit her up for a sale.

"LinkedIn is also very handy for people networking to look for jobs. It's a great backdoor connection."

"So if I was looking for customers who are professionals working in a corporate environment, I might want to use LinkedIn as my social media network of choice."

"You are correct. Plus, there are lots of great niche groups in LinkedIn. It never hurts to connect with peers in your field of interest, as well as with new customers."

"True, true," muses Emily. "What about YouTube? Is that a tool I can use to grow Gino's?"

"Most people only know YouTube as a video-hosting website. What people don't realize is that YouTube is the number two search engine in the world and that it's also owned by Google.

"Because Apple does not support Flash, millions of website owners are forced to convert their videos and host them on YouTube so they can be seen by mobile users. This means that there are millions upon millions of searches done on YouTube every day. If you have a product or service that is unique, you can make mini TV ads and post them on YouTube so that when people search, yours might come up as a related video.

"Also, when people do searches for common keywords, YouTube videos will often show up in the results. A smart marketer can use YouTube to promote awareness of her products to people who are just doing general searches. You know how a picture tells a thousand words? Well, a YouTube video can do in one minute what a whole long sales page of text might do if people read it. A video is often an easier point of entry. Reading a sales letter on a website may be daunting to time-impoverished people, yet who can't commit to watching thirty to sixty seconds of video?

"You can even pay YouTube to have your ad featured and promoted as a sponsored ad while people are looking at other videos."

"So what you are saying is that if I have a video I want to show on my website, it is best to have it converted to YouTube and have it shown from YouTube's server. This way I could get additional people seeing it just because YouTube has so much traffic. This is particularly helpful if my video is relevant to other people's searches, especially since people are more likely to watch a quick video than commit to reading a lot of text on a site."

Kat smiles as she picks up her mobile phone. "That's correct." She stabs at the screen a few times and looks up at Emily. "While I can talk about social media all day long, I do have to meet with another department in a couple of minutes. I just received a text from Mark that he is on his way up in the elevator. Why don't you wait here for a few minutes? Mark will be here in a minute or two and would love to go through some of the basics of mobile marketing with you."

"Thanks, Kat, you've been great." They both rise and hug. "I truly owe you. Think of those nachos as a down payment. Would you like to come over for dinner later this week? I'll make my famous Moroccan chicken tagine for you."

"Sounds delish! I'll bring some white wine. Just relax for a moment. Mark should be right in. I've got to dash. Catch you later!" Kat grabs her phone and walks out the door. Emily sits down on the couch, picks up her phone, and checks her messages. While reading her e-mails, she receives a text message from Taco Loco. It says, "We're having a slow night. Come join us. Nachos for only $2 (normally $9.95). Tonight only. VIP only."

Emily wonders briefly how Taco Loco got her phone number to send her this offer; then she remembers that earlier that day, while at Taco Loco, she sent a text message to the special short code number to get a free drink. This must have added her to Taco Loco's list, and Taco Loco just sent an SMS broadcast to everyone on its VIP list to invite them to come to dinner tonight for discounted nachos.

Emily thinks to herself, "Very clever. I should definitely remember this and do the same for Gino's when I get back." Just then Mark enters the office with a big smile. "Hi, Emily. Kat told me that you were waiting for me to give you a walk-through on mobile marketing. Are you ready to get started?"

"Absolutely!" Emily smiles in return.

"Excellent! So am I. I was meeting with the owners of the local theater and absolutely couldn't resist the smell of the fresh popcorn. Dig in."

"Brilliant, thanks!" Emily and Mark both scoop a handful of popcorn out of the bag and settle onto the couch.

CHAPTER 11

EMILY LEARNS THE DOS AND DON'TS OF MOBILE MARKETING

"Emily, before we dive into mobile marketing, I would like to give you a few basic principles—the dos and don'ts of the biz," Mark says. "This will make it easier for you to understand how to put together a mobile marketing strategy for Gino's when you do it yourself."

"I'm all ears."

"Mobile marketing can be divided into two categories: **list-acquisition activities** and **list-monetization activities**. Do you want to take a crack at figuring out what these two things mean?"

Emily thinks about it for a minute and recalls Miguel's VIP club and her recent message about the two-dollar nachos. "Earlier today I saw Taco Loco's invitation to join the VIP club. All I had to do was send a text message to the special short code phone number with the words 'freedrinks' to receive a free drink. I guess this is how I was entered into Taco Loco's VIP database. So this must be what you call a list-acquisition activity."

Mark smiles. "Correct. So what's a list monetization activity?"

"A few moments ago, I received a message from Taco Loco for a special offer for some nachos. An order normally costs nine ninety-five but will cost only two dollars tonight. I would imagine that that would be a list-monetization activity. Taco Loco is enticing me to come in tonight because it is having a slow day. The way I see it, everyone wins. I get inexpensive nachos but, chances are, I will also be ordering an alcoholic drink or two and perhaps even a salad. Taco Loco wins because I will be spending money there instead of eating at home."

"You've got it. So to be successful in mobile marketing, you have to focus on these two things all the time—first, how to grow your list and keep it, and, second, how to make money from that list. While this may sound easy, there are actually a few common sense things to keep in mind.

"You have to have a general understanding of what the lifetime value of your customer is. For example, if someone opts to become a client of Gino's, how much is that client worth over the next ten years to your company?"

Emily ponders that and says, "Jeez, Mark, I have no idea. That's so hard to figure out. Why is that so important anyway?"

"It's not as hard to figure out as you think," Mark reassures her." Let's start with a few questions. How many times a month would an average customer order from you?"

"About two to three times a month, on average."

"When a customer comes in and eats at your restaurant, how much profit do you make?"

"On average, including kids and drinks, we make about forty dollars per family."

"Let's do the math," Mark says. "Two to three times a month equates to about two and a half times per client. Fair enough?"

"That's fair."

"So if each family comes in two and a half times a month and you earn forty dollars from that family, then you make about a hundred dollars per family. So over a twelve-month period, every family is worth twelve hundred dollars, and over a ten-year period, that family is worth twelve thousand dollars."

Emily objects and says, "Wait a minute, Mark, that's a gross generalization. Not every client who may opt in behaves this way."

"You are correct. But this gives us a very rough idea about the lifetime worth of a customer that we didn't have before. So let's say that in the worst-case scenario, only one in ten people become that ideal customer. If we divide twelve thousand dollars by ten, we will get twelve hundred dollars. Correct?"

Emily nods, "Correct, and yes, that's a fair assumption."

"So what we have is a value of about twelve hundred dollars per client over the estimated life of the customer. Of course this number differs from business to business, but the basic idea remains the same," says Mark as he grabs another handful of popcorn.

"I still don't understand the point of this."

"Em, let me ask you this. If every time you gave me a dollar, I gave you two dollars back, how many times would you want to do that?"

Emily smiles. "All day long, Mark! If you are willing to double my money every time I give it to you, I would keep on doing it until you say stop."

"Exactly! That's why we need to know the lifetime value [LTV] of the customer. Once we know that a lead is worth about twelve hundred dollars for Gino's, we know that if we spend any money that is less than twelve hundred dollars to get that lead, we will be ahead of the game and be profitable."

"Wow, that's amazing. I had never thought of it like that before. Is that the reason why life insurance companies pay hundreds of dollars for leads?"

"That's exactly why. Insurance companies know that once someone buys an insurance policy, the chances that person will leave is very slim, and they've calculated the value of that customer over the life of the client.

"Let's be even more conservative. If we were to spend anything less than a hundred and twenty dollars per lead, would you agree that over the next few years, Gino's would be ahead of the game, on average?"

"Well, assuming that people don't deviate their behavior from our past history, I would have to agree with you, considering you've cut the estimation by a factor of ten."

Mark responds, "With a magic number of a hundred and twenty dollars, we have a lot of room to be creative. We can offer to give that client all sorts of incentives to entice her to come to Gino's or to opt in to Gino's VIP database. Correct?"

Emily nods. "Correct."

"Are you familiar with a concept called a 'loss leader,' Em?" asks Mark.

"Yes, I am familiar with that concept," Emily sputters. "I've bought enough cheap printers in my life to be familiar with that. Printer manufacturers realized that the money is in selling people cartridges that quickly dry and deteriorate and not the printer itself. They typically sell their printers at a loss so they can recoup their money by selling overpriced print cartridges."

"Jeez, Em, you sound a little angry and bitter." Mark grins.

Emily raises her voice in mock rage. "No, not at all. I'm not bitter. But there is a reason why I only use laser printers."

"So, if you know the lifetime value of your customer, you will be able to calculate special loss-leader offers and other incentives to encourage them to join your list."

"Yes, Mark—thanks to you."

"Great, so let's talk about more list-acquisition activities. You've seen Taco Loco offering great incentives to convince people to opt in. I'm sure you can plan something similar for Gino's. I'm assuming you've also heard from Kat about doing a cross-promotion strategy in which you hook up with a nonprofit and offer to donate x dollars per person who opts in to your VIP list.

"In the past I have also used weekly prize drawings. Usually the winner receives twenty-five dollars' worth of food at your restaurant or a gift card.

"You could work in conjunction with another restaurant, like Taco Loco, and cross-promote each other in a sort of 'you scratch my back, I'll scratch yours' type of arrangement. Basically the sky's the limit. It is only limited by your imagination."

"What are some things I should be aware of?" Emily asks. "What are the no-nos of mobile marketing?"

Mark smiles. "I'm glad you asked. There are a few things that you should not do in mobile marketing.

"Make sure you first build value to your list. Businesses need to understand that people have given them *conditional* permission to send offers to them. This is not an open invitation for unlimited spam. Keep in mind that many people have to pay to receive texts on a per-message basis. Right now in the United States, this is around twenty cents a message, unless you are on an unlimited SMS plan. This means that every time a business sends an offer to that client, it is costing the client twenty cents. That message better be worth more than twenty cents in value to the client for that person to stay on your list. Of course, we're talking about averages. Ideally, your SMS broadcasts should be timely special offers that are well worth the while for the receivers to entice them to stay on your list.

"Your message needs to have a specific call to action. We spoke about a call to action earlier. You'll be surprised how many people send out SMS broadcasts with no calls to action. If you don't tell people what to do, they will not do it. For example, tell people that in order to enjoy this special, they have to come in tonight—and tonight only.

"Your offer should have a time urgency factor to keep things fresh and exciting. You'd be amazed how many times businesses send out an SMS broadcast that says something like, 'As a VIP client, just come in and receive a twenty-five percent discount.' While this is great, there is room for confusion. Is the twenty-five percent for today? Next week? Next year? There is no urgency.

"Timing is also very important. You are in the food business, and if you want people to come to your restaurant for dinner, sending your offer between three and five p.m. would be more effective than, say, seven in the morning. Or if you were an accountant, sending out an offer in mid-January might yield a better result than a June offer.

"Always avoid **spam**. So many businesses that are new to mobile marketing are so infatuated with the power and technology that they forget the basics of human decency. In their hearts and minds, they know that sending unsolicited messages to people is unwelcome and ineffective. Always think carefully before you ally yourself with other marketers and send message to their lists. You may hear things like, 'Come, send to our list! We have over a million names in our database. They are all opt-ins.' These sorts of things are dangerous. We know from <u>Permission Marketing</u> (credit to Seth Godin's book) that permission is not transferable. What this means is that if you opted in to Taco Loco's VIP offer, then you only gave Taco Loco permission to send offers to you. If Taco Loco sells your information to Bob the dentist, and Bob sends an offer to you, you would not be very happy. You did not give Bob permission to send you offers. The same goes for buying names or lists. It's not ethical, nor is it welcomed, and consequently, it is not very effective, either.

"Another thing to be conscious of is **list exhaustion**. List exhaustion is when you over-solicit your people with offers. People just get sick of hearing from you."

"Wow, that's something I never thought about."

"On the other hand—and this is just as deadly—there is something called list boredom. **List boredom** is the opposite of list exhaustion in that you don't solicit your list enough, and they forget about you. Worse still, they forget they ever gave you permission to send them offers and start accusing you of sending them unsolicited spam."

"Wow, Mark, I had no idea. I'm glad I've been able to talk with you first before engaging in my mobile media campaign. I want to revisit what you said earlier about the cost to the receiver of my SMS broadcasts. From what you are saying, I need to constantly remind myself that, before I send out an offer, I should make sure I am sending out something new, exciting, or worthwhile to my users."

"That's right, Em. There's yet another caution I have for you. It's called the '**Pavlov Effect.**'"

"Isn't that some sort of psychological experiment involving a dog?" asks Emily.

Mark laughs and says, "Yes. The term comes from a famous Russian physiologist named Ivan Pavlov. He conducted an experiment in which he would ring a bell before giving his dog a meal. What he found was that after a while, every time he would ring the bell, his dog would salivate—even without the food being present. At the time, it was a huge discovery. This phenomenon is called 'conditioning.'

"This also applies to mobile marketing. We have to be careful not to train our customers to be so dependent on our special offers that they stop their casual behavior. Let me explain. Let's say every Wednesday, because it's traditionally slow at the restaurant on Wednesdays, you make a habit of sending a special offer for a really discounted meal, like a five-dollar steak dinner or a two-dollar pizza, to encourage people to come in the door. After a while you will get a certain group of people who will no longer come to your restaurant unless it is on a Wednesday evening. You've inadvertently conditioned your customers to be just like Pavlov's dog."

Shocked by this, Emily exclaims, "Mark, you've just pretty much thrown everything you've taught me out the window. On the one hand, you said to make sure I provide value to my list, and then on the other hand, you said to not condition them. I'm getting confused."

"As a list owner, you have to walk a fine line between offering great deals and making your deals predictable. The trick is to mix it up so that your offers are less predictable."

Breathing a sigh of relief, Emily says, "Yes, I guess that's the key. I should mix up my offers so that customers can still be spontaneous. Thank you for that great pointer, Mark."

"Em, so that I know you are following me, would you please summarize what we've talked about thus far?"

"I would love to. One of the things I need to find out is what the lifetime value of a customer is for Gino's. It's not an exact science, but even having a rough idea will enable us to make smart marketing decisions and make break-even analysis decisions on how much we can afford to pay to acquire a new patron. We can combine this knowledge with what you call a 'loss leader' so that we can entice our customers to come try our food and restaurant.

"We have to be conscious and respectful of the people who have given their permission to market to them. Permission is not transferable, and it's just bad to spam people, even if the people who try to sell us their marketing services tell us it's OK to do so. We need to strive to make sure what we send to our people is of value to woo them so they are less inclined to withdraw from our list. At the same time, we have to mix up our offers so that our customers do not come to depend on our offers as the only times they come to eat at Gino's.

"You spoke about two types of activities in mobile marketing—list-acquisition activities and list-monetization activities. Thus far, you've primarily focused on list-acquisition activities. I guess you'll talk to me about list-monetization activities next?" Emily asks hopefully.

CHAPTER 12

EMILY LEARNS LIST MONETIZATION STRATEGIES

"Before we go too much deeper into list-monetization strategies," Mark begins, "let me explain another mobile technology to you. It's called an autoresponder.

"An autoresponder does what its name implies. It automatically 'responds' to an SMS message. For example, let's say you begin a mobile marketing plan with us and we've assigned you a short code of five-five-five-five-five and a keyword of 'freedrinks.' When clients send a text message to your short code with that keyword, they will see an automatic response that either welcomes them to the VIP club or some other message of your choosing. This is an example of an autoresponder.

"You can also have your autoresponder send out other messages, such as a coupon code or any other messages, and even include a link to your website."

"OK, that makes sense. So?"

"But wait, there's more. You can be even more clever in your use of autoresponders by creating what we call a sequential SMS autoresponder. Imagine if when you opt in to Taco Loco's database, you are registered to receive a series of automatic messages, meaning that once a week or so, a new offer is sent to your phone. Imagine if this offer is set up automatically for the next two years."

Stunned, Emily says, "So let me get this straight. If I opt in to Taco Loco, I could potentially be receiving an offer every week from Taco Loco for the next two years? And no one at Taco Loco actually lifts a finger? It just comes to me automatically?"

"Affirmative."

Emily exclaims, "Wow, this goes hand in hand with what we spoke about earlier with the LTV of a customer. If we can set up a series so that once someone opts in to Gino's VIP club, that person regularly receives offers every week or two, we could have the person come back to us for years to come. And unlike traditional advertising, which costs us money every time we have an impression or ad view, with this strategy, our only cost is the price of sending out an SMS message."

"In addition to receiving regular offers, you can even send out the occasional broadcast to your members when you have a sale or special event," Mark adds.

"I see what you mean by a monetization strategy. This is very powerful. As far as creating these special offers, is there anything I need to know?"

"Well, Em, it's not rocket science. The thing you want to keep in mind is to give something that is of high perceived value to your customer yet has a low cost to you. In Gino's case, it might be soft drinks, bread sticks, garlic bread, etcetera. In the case of a dentist, it might be discounted cleanings or free teeth whitening.

From time to time, you might want to give discounts on your main products, but that varies from situation to situation.

"Always remember to add some fun into your marketing. It may sound silly, but too often business is too serious. People like to be entertained, so be sure to tell stories. Make things up. Use your imagination. Let me give you an example. As you recall, we told the story of how Miguel decided to divert his marketing budget and give the money to his customers. That's a story. He posted the story everywhere in his store. He also had his employees tell that story to his customers.

"Another story you could use might be that Maria has made a bet. If we were able to get x number of people to come to her birthday event at the restaurant, she will buy everyone drinks.

"The point is, use your imagination. Have fun. One of the things that make mobile devices great is that they are also entertainment devices, so don't forget to entertain. It is always better if you can make them smile.

"One of the things that we found to be very successful for Taco Loco was to encourage their employees to get involved in talking up the VIP club. If your employees think it is a great idea and of great value, then your customers will be more inclined to join.

"I remember overhearing a conversation one of Taco Loco's waitresses had with a customer. The customer asked the waitress, 'If I send an SMS, am I going to get spammed to death? I don't have an unlimited SMS plan, you know.' The waitress responds by saying, 'No, it's actually quite awesome. I have gotten a lot of my friends to join. They come in all the time because of the specials they receive. For example, just last night we had two-dollar nachos night. These are normally nine ninety-five.' Needless to say, the customer decided to join Taco Loco's VIP club despite her limited SMS plan."

"Thanks, Mark! I will be sure to remember to train our staff about our offers or the benefits of our VIP club."

"You should also create posters and signs to describe the benefits of your VIP club and have them prominently displayed so people can see them. In Gino's case, since you are both a restaurant and a pizza-delivery business, you can put this information on each table in one of those tent displays as well as on your pizza boxes."

"I noticed," remarks Emily, "that Taco Loco also puts the benefits right on the menu. I'm definitely going to recommend that we redo our menu to include descriptions of the benefits of our soon-to-be VIP club."

Standing up, Mark says, "Well, Em, I've given you some of the basics, and we've eaten all the popcorn. I've got to finish some things at my desk before I go home for the evening. Why don't you ponder what I've given you today, and maybe we can meet later this week to discuss how we can implement a SoMo strategy for Gino's."

"Thank you for your time, Mark. I will definitely think about what we discussed and get back to you."

Emily walks back to her office, nearly overwhelmed by all the information Kat and Mark shared with her. She sits at her desk and opens her notebook. She begins distilling her notes into action lists. As she organizes her thoughts and her to-dos, a plan begins to form.

CHAPTER 13

EMILY MEETS ANNIE THE ACCOUNTANT

The next day, refreshed after a good night's sleep, Emily begins to contact Maria's list of other business owners currently using mobile marketing to promote their business. She makes an appointment with Annie for that afternoon. Annie is Maria's accountant. She then spends her morning working on her action lists and thinking about who in the company would be best suited for each item. Before she realizes it, it's past lunch. Emily stops at a café on the way to Annie's office and notices how many people are *not* utilizing mobile and social marketing ideas. She is grinning as she reaches Annie's door.

"Annie, thank you so much for spending the time to talk to me about your mobile marketing campaign."

"It's my pleasure, Emily. Maria has been a long-time client of mine, and I'm always happy to help."

"Annie, I saw you on the news recently. You were helping to raise some money for a local nonprofit. Could you tell me a bit more about that?"

Annie laughs. "That was the culmination of a long marketing campaign we put together with Help the Children and Homes for Pets.[4] Both of these nonprofits are clients of mine. I do the books for them. We decided to work together to increase our exposure in the news together.

"We started with a story. I wanted to donate a thousand dollars to a nonprofit but could not decide which to give the money to. I wanted people's help in deciding which I should choose. The organization with the most votes received the money.

"I approached both nonprofit organizations and talked to their publicity people. We created three press releases that we sent all over town. Of course, this benefits the nonprofits either way, as both would receive a lavish amount of publicity and, as a result, donations. Our donation would just be the frosting on a delicious, delicious cake for one of them.

"Before I started the event, I had to build a mobile-friendly website. Our site was woefully out of date. I created it years ago and never had the time to update it."

"Why did you need to update your website to be mobile friendly?"

"For one thing, it was not mobile friendly at all. It was hard for customers to see information quickly from my old site. For another, I wanted to make my website readily accessible to people using their smartphones so they know my hours of operation and

---

4   These are fictional nonprofit organizations and have no connection with any NPOs that happen to have the same name.

address and could see connections to my social media properties. I remember a long-term client who phoned very frustrated a few months ago because she was trying to refer a new client to me while they were at lunch. All they had were mobile phones, and my site was so archaic that they couldn't contact me in the moment. She had to wait until she returned to her office to forward my information to her friend. I almost lost a new client because of my old site. Plus, I wanted to make it possible for people to vote for which nonprofit to support right from both my desktop and mobile websites."

"So where and how did you make your mobile website?" Emily asks.

Annie responds, "I just went to Mango Tree Mobile. The company referred me to a designer to redo my desktop site and then took the information and logos from my existing website and delivered my mobile website to me within a couple of days. I then told Mango Tree Mobile what to fix that was out of date, and within a couple days, the company delivered exactly what I wanted. What's great is that I was charged a very reasonable fixed price for the service. The company did not nickel and dime me to death, and I did not have to spend mental effort to manage the project. Also, since the company's consultants specialize in this stuff, they knew to hook up all my social media properties to my mobile website for me. The whole time, I was doing what I'm best at—accounting. I didn't have to stress over any of the techie stuff.

"Next, I created a mobile SMS voting campaign that simply tracked how many people opted in to one of my two lists."

"How did you do that? Did that involve setting up a couple of keywords or something?"

"That is exactly what I did. I created two keywords: children and pets. My call to action was simple. I asked people to vote by sending their SMS to five-five-five-five-five with the message of 'children' if they thought I should support Help the Children or 'pets' if they thought I should support Homes for Pets."

"How did you come up with a thousand dollars? Did you calculate that by some sort of lifetime value for your customer?"

"No. My company had budgeted that amount already for advertising. We just wanted to do something fun and creative. This strategy worked for us because accounting is somewhat of a universal product in that almost everyone needs to file a tax return. If my company was more specialized, like a business specializing in carpentry or plumbing, this strategy might not have worked very well.

Emily concludes, "So by undertaking this campaign, you were able to entice quite a few people to join your list as a list-acquisition strategy through the use of free publicity because you did a nonprofit tie-in."

Annie nods. "Not only that, we also had a great deal of social media participation. I also worked with the publicist of each of the nonprofits to teach them to promote to their members. Particularly, I had them ask their members to spread the news via Facebook."

"Wow, Annie, that's unbelievable! You tied nonprofits, mobile marketing, and social media into your marketing? You should have been in marketing and not accountancy."

Annie laughs. "Well, you have my father to thank for that. He wanted his little girl to grow up to have a career that makes money. Yes, I worked with a marketing company to create two images—one for each nonprofit. The picture says 'Help spread the word. Vote for Help the Children. Please send an SMS message to 55555 with the word *children*. If we receive the most votes, we will receive $1,000 from our donor, Annie's Accounting. Please share.' We made the same one for Homes for Pets. We had their supporters post this picture on their Facebook updates and ask their friends to share. This spread pretty well, and I had an influx of new clients because people who support nonprofits tend to flock to others who share their choices."

"That's understandable. I feel the same. How did you know it worked? Were you able to count how many times the picture was shared?"

"Yes. Facebook keeps track and reports on how many times a picture has been shared and commented on. Anyway, we ended up with over twelve hundred votes, and Homes for Pets won. I invited the press out, and the local TV station even ran a story about the event. That's why you saw me on TV giving the check to Patricia from Homes for Pets.

"I ended up paying less than a dollar per opt-in to my database. Now I can send out a few blasts a year near tax time to get people to use me for their accounting needs. I have it all automated in a sequential SMS autoresponder to send follow-ups for special offers every year for the next ten years.

"What's more, I no longer need to advertise in the *Yellow Pages* or the newspaper to get additional business. I also improve my social equity because people equate me as a good person since I have helped nonprofit organizations. Of course, that's a side benefit. I would support these organizations anyway, but having my name associated with being a supporter of nonprofits doesn't hurt my brand image."

"So let me get this straight," Emily says. "You used an SMS competition as your list-acquisition strategy by working with a couple of nonprofits. You were able to pull this off by telling a story that sells. It was successful because you showed the local nonprofits that they would also benefit from this event through increased awareness, even if they did not win the prize.

"As your list-monetization strategy, you can now send offers for discounts for your services a few times a year. You created a sequential SMS autoresponder so that your offer is sent out automatically, year after year, to the people on your list."

Annie nods. "Emily, you are quick. That's a great way to summarize it."

Emily thanks Annie. As she leaves the building, she notices a large, framed photo of Annie and a giant check for a thousand dollars being handed to a woman holding a small, fluffy dog. Emily's mind is swirling with ideas for great photos Gino's could be hanging on the walls in the not-too-distant future as she walks to her next appointment with Maggie, Maria's massage therapist.

CHAPTER 14

EMILY MEETS MAGGIE THE MASSAGE THERAPIST

Maggie greets Emily warmly and offers Emily some tea as they sit down together in what has to be one of the coziest waiting rooms Emily has ever seen. Soft lighting and scented candles are used in combination with relaxing colors and comfy furniture. Clearly, Maggie knows how to relax her clients.

Emily accepts a mug of berry-scented tea from Maggie. "How did you and Maria meet?" she begins.

Maggie smiles and answers, "Well, that's an interesting story. I've only been at this for about six months, and Maria was one of my first customers. When I first graduated from massage school, I knew nothing about marketing. I didn't even have a website."

"So if you knew nothing about marketing, how did you end up filling your clinic?"

"When I started, I had no clients. I had nothing. The only thing I really had was time—lots and lots of free time that I used that as an asset to grow my business."

"How is having free time an asset?"

"Well, because I had lots of open spaces and other therapists didn't, I could be flexible with what hours I made myself available and how much I could charge. I signed up with Mango Tree Mobile's marketing program. I was offered a free coaching program to learn about mobile marketing. With Mango Tree Mobile, I was given a short code and I created a keyword for my ads."

"I created what they call a 'no-brainer offer.' I gave away my massage services for ten dollars an hour. Other therapists in my area charge between sixty to ninety dollars per hour."

Emily exclaims, "Maggie, that's crazy! How could you afford to do that?"

"Well, let's put it this way: if I were to go out and get a job in this economy, chances are, I would be earning just over ten dollars an hour, anyway. I figured I had nothing to lose. If I was booked end to end, I would still be making a decent living. I used this special pricing as a 'loss leader.'"

Emily nods. "Oh yeah, I am familiar with the loss-leader concept. You lose money in the beginning of the relationship because you know that over a long period, you will make more money by acquiring the client."

"That's correct. I happen to be really good with sports injuries—it's kind of my specialty. I figured that I would get a few customers who are athletes who might need my services in the future. You know how sports enthusiasts are—they love the activity, so they are likely to continue doing it and need someone to keep their bodies ticking. I have several clients now who come in for monthly 'tune-ups,' whether they think they have an issue or not. They are my bread and butter now.

"Once I created my keyword and offer, I placed an ad both in the classifieds section of the local newspaper and in the dining section. I also ran a few ads on the radio about my ten-dollar massage. The ad went like this: 'Stressed out? Need a massage? For a ten-dollar one-hour massage, send an SMS to five-five-five-five-five with the words '10massage.'

"Because it was such a no-brainer, I had quite a few people opt in to my offer. This was how I was introduced to Maria. She was one of the people who opted in to my ten-dollar massage offer.

"In my control panel with Mango Tree Mobile, I was able to set up an autoresponder that sends back instructions for my opt-in users to come to my mobile website to book their appointments automatically."

"Wait a minute," Emily interjects. "These people opted in to your offer and then booked a session with you without even talking to you?"

"Yes. I had Mango Tree Mobile set up a link from my site to online appointment-scheduling software. This system even sends follow-ups and reminders for people who schedule themselves. With Mango Tree Mobile, I can schedule an SMS follow-up message to make sure my clients show up."

Emily accepts a refill of delicious tea from Maggie. "So how well did the campaign work for you?"

Maggie smiles sheepishly. "Let's put it this way: I only work when I want to these days. I can have my schedule fully booked for two weeks out of every month and I can take two weeks off to chill."

"How?"

"I send SMS broadcasts to invite my clients to book with me for a discount. I also sell them prepackaged discount plans—for example, buy five, get one free if you pay in advance. Whenever I am free, I run broadcasts like 'I am free today. Thirty-five-dollar-an-hour massage, only for the first ten people. Today only.'"

"Wow, that's neat. Aren't you afraid of conditioning your customers to only come to you when you have these discounts?"

"Well, for one thing, I send these promotions sporadically, so they cannot predict when I will make these offers. For another, it is on a first-come, first-served basis. And if I fill ten spots for thirty-five dollars a pop, that's enough to feed me. That's better than two clients a day at fifty dollars an hour. I would rather be busy than sitting idly and staring at the phone."

"Is there anything else you do to promote your business?" Emily asks.

"I also had Mango Tree Mobile set up my social media profiles. I'm on Google Maps, Yelp, Foursquare, and Facebook. After each massage, I ask my clients to give me a review on these social media sites. In the beginning I offered to reduce the bill by five dollars if they did. They would write the review right then and take the discount immediately."

"But that's crazy. You might end up giving your massages for free!"

"Not really. Even if I earned nothing, I earned social equity. I now have a bunch of reviews on these social media properties. In fact, I now have the most reviews for massage therapists in town, and most of mine are rated very highly. Essentially, for five dollars, I am getting years' worth of free advertising."

"So let me get this straight. You went to Mango Tree Mobile and had the company set up your mobile website. You also had it help create your social media profiles for you. Then it linked your social media properties back to your mobile website. You now use Mango Tree Mobile to manage your SMS opt-ins and SMS broadcasts. Is that right?"

Maggie nods. "It's nice to be able to just go to one shop that does everything. The company even provides me with a free coaching program to help me formulate my marketing strategies. And since the consultants specialize in this sort of business, they are able to do it quickly, affordably, and professionally.

"If you compare my marketing strategy to how other massage therapists market their business, I am way ahead of the game. I will run those ten-dollar special offers only once in a while, when I am running low on bookings, and then I just keep running occasional promotions to get clients to come see me, especially when I am not busy.

"As a result of my marketing—especially all those reviews on places like Google Maps, Yelp, and Facebook—I am getting additional exposure through social media, as well as natural searches through Google and Microsoft Bing.

"Through these viral strategies and social media, I've been able to get myself established and get free referrals from businesses without needing to advertise."

"That's really cool, Maggie. I'm impressed. You've been able to combine the use of both mobile marketing and social media to drive traffic. I like how you were willing to invest in your future growth and social equity by 'paying' your customers to write reviews for you. This has set you apart from many other therapists in your area. Way to go!"

"Thank you, Emily."

With that, Emily thanks Maggie, finishes her tea, and reluctantly leaves the luxurious comfort of Maggie's waiting room to return to her own, by comparison, hard and unwelcoming office chair. She compiles more action lists based on the day's interviews. She also takes a moment to confirm with Richie, a successful local real estate agent, her appointment for the next morning.

As she leaves the office and heads home, Emily laments, "I should have asked Maggie where she buys her furniture. I wonder if she does interior decorating consulting, as well as massages."

CHAPTER 15

EMILY MEETS RICHIE THE REAL ESTATE AGENT

Bright and early the next morning, Richie appears outside Emily's office right on time. Emily hops into his car and notices the two steaming hot lattes in the cup holders between the seats. She chooses one of the warm croissants and offers Richie the bag with the other.

"Good morning! Thanks for spending the time to show me around and teach me how you have been using mobile marketing, Richie," Emily says.

"No problem, Emily. This one is the soy latte for you," he says, pointing to one cup. "And thanks for the croissant. Let's go take a look at one of my properties, and I'll share some of my tactics with you. Maria has sent plenty of her friends my way over the years. This is the least I could do."

They munch companionably and sip coffee as they drive just outside of the city to a nice property with a gorgeous magnolia tree in full bloom. Emily notes the 'for sale' sign with Richie's name on it by the curb.

Richie exits the car and motions for Emily to follow him. "Come take a look at this sign, Emily. What do you see?"

Emily examines the sign for a minute and says, "Well, for one thing, I don't see a price anywhere. There is a QR code in the corner, and it says that I can find more information about the property by sending an SMS message to five-five-five-five-five with the keyword '123jeffersonst.'"

Richie smiles. "That's right, Emily. My company has embraced mobile marketing in a big way. We realize that more and more people these days use their cell phones to look for houses. Remember how, in days of old, there were piles and piles of paper brochures? We had no idea who took them. There was no way for us to follow up with them. With the use of mobile technology, we are able to be a lot more proactive about showing houses for our clients. Here, let me show you.

Please bring out your phone and scan that QR code on the property's listing board."

Emily takes out her iPhone and scans the QR code. Within a few seconds, she gets a response with the message, "Thank you for your interest. For more info, come to http://www.richieproperties. com/123jefferesonst." Emily then clicks on the link and is quickly presented with a description page about the property, including a video walk-through.

Emily also notices that Richie received a text message with Emily's phone number a moment after she submitted her text.

Richie shows Emily his phone. "See? When you scanned in the QR code with your phone, I had it programmed to send an SMS to my short code with the keyword '123jeffersonst.' I have also set up an autoresponder that responds to that particular keyword to send back the link for the property's mobile listing page. The system is also set to notify me immediately," he says, pointing to his screen, "when someone opts in. I now know that someone is in front of the house *right now*. I know that if I call the person within the next five minutes, I am much more likely to catch him or her, strike up a conversation, and possibly even go out and meet the person at the property.

"In the real estate business, it is always good to strike while the iron is hot, and nothing impresses clients more than when I am able to call them while they are right in front of the property. This saves everybody time, as the potential buyer does not have to wait or schedule an appointment.

"I also score big points from sellers. Every week I can make a report showing them how many times someone has seen their house through my SMS autoresponder tracking system."

Emily nods. "Wow, that's pretty neat. This reminds me of the last time I was at a car lot. It was late, and I was just looking around with Kat after walking to the car from the movies. Anyway, we noticed a QR code on the window. So out of curiosity, Kat scanned in the QR code with her phone and got the same thing. She was sent to a page listing the car's details and history. The next day, I think she received a follow-up phone call from the car lot asking if she had any further questions. I had no idea how they did it at the time, yet I was impressed."

"Yes, we love this new technology," Richie says. "It just makes it a lot easier for us to help buyers find the house they are looking for."

Emily pauses for a moment. "At the same time, that can be pretty creepy. As a girl, I am somewhat concerned about my privacy. I just want to know the price of the property and don't want to be harassed."

Richie nods. "That's perfectly understandable. We get that concern all the time. We always make a point of explaining to buyers that we are just giving them a courtesy follow-up call. We are not harassing them, nor are they obliged to meet with us. The same goes both ways. We are only interested in showing the house to genuinely interested buyers anyway. Casual buyers often do not follow through, but it is nice to have that option of calling clients while they are in front of the property and offering to show it to them right there and then."

"That makes sense. How have sales been since you've been using this method?"

"They've actually been noticeably better. I still have clients who I drive from property to property, but I now have additional targeted inquiries from people on the spot. I was never before able to capture them and now have a chance to introduce interested parties to the houses I have listed. Not all are truly in the market, yet I can easily and quickly determine who is by just a phone call. I don't mind jumping into the car to show a house on a Sunday morning when I know someone really wants to see it. It's always rewarding when I match a home to people who I may never have known were interested before mobile marketing."

Richie drops Emily back at her office. Emily pulls out her phone, checks her e-mail and messages, and drives back to her own house. Her next interview will be with Peter, who owns the local pet shop, and for that, Emily intends to bring her own dog. As she pulls into her driveway, she sees a wet, little nose pressing against the living room window.

CHAPTER 16

EMILY MEETS PETER THE PET SHOP OWNER

Emily and her dog, Jacks, step into Peter's Pet Shop. Emily waves to Peter.

"Hi, Emily. It's nice to see you again. How's my friend Jacks?" he asks as he bends down to scratch behind the dog's ears.

"He's great, feisty as ever. How are things with you?"

"It's going quite well. I take it from your message yesterday that this is more than a kibble run? Here, pull up a stool, and we'll have a chat about some of my mobile marketing strategies."

Gleefully, Emily says, "Oh, do tell! I'm all ears."

Peter offers Jacks a biscuit and explains, "We recently ran a promotion where if a pet owner came into our shop and joined as a VIP member, not only would they be in the list to receive discounts and special offers from us, they would also receive a free can of dog or cat food just by opting in. Needless to say, this worked quite well. Almost everyone who came in decided to join. After all, who can say no to free food?"

They both laugh in agreement.

"When I first moved to town, I didn't know anyone," Emily says. "I used Yelp to find a good pet shop. I came to this shop because there were a lot of positive reviews and you were relatively close to my house. Jacks love a walk where there is a biscuit reward both going and returning. How did you get so many reviews?"

"Well, I bribed them, of course," Peter jokes. "OK, maybe not bribed, but I offered them a can of food for every review they wrote for me. I always made sure I told my customers that they were only obliged to write the truth. Almost everyone wrote good reviews because as a small business owner, I make it my point to get to know my customers and have a good relationship with them.

"I have invested about a couple hundred dollars in pet food giveaways, but as a result, I've been getting more and more business from people who are mobile users. When people search for a pet store near them, they find me. One of the best investments I made was to use Mango Tree Mobile's Mango Social service."

"I've been hearing a lot about Mango Tree Mobile as I speak to small business owners about mobile media. It seems to specialize in helping small businesses get on the mobile marketing bandwagon. What's the Mango Social program?"

Peter laughs. "Actually, Mango Tree Mobile literally put my business on the map. In addition to setting me up with a mobile-friendly website, it also helped me put my business on a bunch of social media sites. I am not very comfortable with all this technology stuff, so it is nice to know I have someone who just takes care of it all for me. Mango Tree Mobile created my Fanpage on Facebook, submitted my information onto Google Maps, and put me onto places like Yelp and Foursquare. It also linked all these properties on my mobile-friendly website so that my customers can simply come to my website and easily go to all these other social media properties directly.

"I don't mean to sound like a walking billboard for Mango Tree Mobile, but its services just make sense. They are reasonably priced, and because the consultants specialize in this stuff, they really know what they are doing.

"I also signed up for the Mango Messaging program. This program gives me a certain number of SMS credits every month so that I can send broadcasts to my list for regular special offers. I also use it to track my member loyalty program."

"What's a member loyalty program? Is it like a VIP club?"

"Yes—for very important pets! As you know, I sell all kinds of supplies for cats and dogs, yet the items that people come back for again and again are the pet foods. So, to encourage people to keep coming back to me, I have a 'buy ten, get one free' deal. Whenever customers buy a can of dog food, I have them use their smartphone to scan a special QR code I have behind my counter."

"What about those who do not have a smartphone?"

"Great question. I use the old-fashioned punch card system. I explain to my customers that it is better to use the smartphone system because it accurately tracks the loyalty purchases. With the punch cards, people often either forget their cards or lose them. I make it easy for them to do whatever is most convenient for them either way.

"With these systems in place, I can make a special large order of one brand or another of pet food and send out an announcement to my VIP list. I make very little on these promotions but know that when my clients come in, they will likely buy other things, like pet toys, leashes, etcetera.

"I then send out an SMS blast to my VIP customers to invite them to participate in my special order. These special prices are reserved for my VIP clients only. I don't even let my regular customers know about the offer; this shows my VIP clients that this is a special benefit I am extending to them as a way of thanking them for their loyalty."

"Wow, that's very smart. It makes a lot of sense," Emily muses. "So you are able to acquire new customers because you have lots of reviews. You received these reviews because you 'paid' your customers in food to write these reviews for you while they were in your shop. You then invited them to join your VIP program by giving away free dog or cat food.

"To monetize your list, you make special orders of pet food in bulk and offer to sell it to them at a vast discount, but only to your VIP members. You also retain their loyalty and track their purchases through a mobile coupon/loyalty program through Mango Tree's Messaging program."

Peter smiles and nods. "That's right."

Emily whips out her iPhone. "Well, I have a very important pet, right Jacks?" Jacks wags his tail enthusiastically. "Let's sign us up for your VIP club. No sensible hound ever turns down food, and no sensible human turns down a discount."

CHAPTER 17

EPILOGUE

(Six months later)

Emily is having lunch with Kat at Gino's to debrief her on her mobile marketing journey.

"Hey there, Em!" Kat leans in to give Emily a hug. "How are things going?"

"Quite well, actually, thanks to you and Mark. Have a seat, and I'll tell you all about it."

After they settle into the booth, their waitress hands them Gino's new menu. The waitress says, "Welcome to Gino's. My name is Rachel, and I will be your waitress today. Today's special is Dracula's Nightmare. It's our own special pizza with extra garlic sauce. It's got enough garlic to dust a vampire. Before taking your order, may I tell you about our VIP program?"

Both Emily and Kat answer with grins, "Sure!"

"When you join our VIP program, you will be put on our special list. We send out notifications for special deals on a regular basis. However, the best part about being a VIP member is that you also participate in our loyalty program. After ten visits to any of Gino's restaurants, you receive a free family-sized pizza. You also are invited to special VIP members-only events that we hold regularly. Might I interest you in joining today?"

Impressed, Kat responds, "Yes. How do I join?"

Rachel answers, "That's easy. See the top right-hand corner of the menu, where it says 'Join our VIP program?' Just either scan the QR code with your smartphone or send a text message to five-five-five-five-five with the keyword 'pizzavip.'"

After taking their orders for drinks, Rachel leaves. Kat brings out her iPhone and scans Gino's QR code for the VIP program. She immediately receives a response welcoming her to the VIP program.

Kat turns to Emily. "Wow, Em, this is great! It seems you've taken what we recommended to heart. What really impresses me is how Rachel was so active in promoting the VIP program."

Emily beams with pride. "Thank you, Kat. We just implemented a few things you taught us, and it's really paying off.

"After I delivered my report to Maria, she promoted me to a special position as the marketing director for the company. We really didn't have anyone managing our marketing, so it was an interesting new responsibility.

"The first thing I did was to call and cancel our *Yellow Pages* ad. We're still listed there, of course, in case some of our older customers still rely on the phone book.

"I did as you suggested. I went to Mango Tree Mobile and joined the free mobile marketing coaching program. It was very helpful.

The staff laid the foundation for me and broke the execution plan into digestible chunks with an action plan in every module. I also love the videos showing me how to set everything up.

"With the money I saved from our *Yellow Pages* ad, I went ahead with the 'Whole Mango' package. I figured it just made sense to save myself the headache of figuring it all out by myself and have the consultants set it all up for me.

"With the package, Mango Tree Mobile created a mobile-friendly version of our website. It has all the features you and Mark were recommending that a mobile website should have.

"The company also set us up on Google Maps and created a Facebook Fanpage for us. It created entries for us on Yelp and Foursquare, as well.

"It also integrated our mobile website with our social media properties for us. We hardly needed to lift a finger, and I didn't have to manage yet another project.

"The best thing about the 'Whole Mango' was the **Done For You Solution**. The team at Mango Tree Mobile interviewed me to find out what I needed and came up with a plan for our SoMo Marketing campaign. They had me fill out a form of what sort of offers I would like to give to our customers and what incentives we are going to offer to get people to opt in to our various marketing programs. *Then they just did it all for us.* I nearly fell out of my chair. Here I thought I would have to sit down and implement all these things and figure it out by myself.

"Mango Tree Mobile, I am embarrassed to say, made my job as the marketing director so freaking easy. I got our new marketing strategy implemented without doing any of the heavy lifting. Maria loves me because she thinks I walk on water. She doesn't know that I actually did very little besides coming up with the strategy and the project management; the rest was all thanks to Mango Tree Mobile.

"After the initial interview, Mango Tree Mobile set up my sequential autoresponders for me to automatically solicit clients who join our VIP program for the next two years.

"I am able to log in to my console at any time I want and send out a special offer whenever we are having a slow day.

"Mango Tree Mobile also created a number of QR codes for us to use, like the QR code you just used to join our VIP program.

"We also use the QR codes for our newspaper and coupon ads now. Remember when we first met about mobile marketing and Mark told me about a call to action?"

"Yes."

"Well, our ads now have a QR code and SMS text messages as a call to action to get our readers to interact with us. As a result, we are able to directly track our ROI to the cent and tell whether our advertising investments yield a positive return on investment.

"We also use these QR codes on our pizza boxes so that people can just pick up our boxes and call us from their smartphones. The funny thing is, we are getting a lot more new clients who are just too lazy to look up the number for their regular pizza restaurants. They see our boxes and just use their smartphone to call us."

Kat smiles broadly. "Wow, this is really cool. I am so glad I could help you with this stuff. Oh, and don't feel bad about not using Mark and me. We were happy to help. To be honest, we've got more work than we know what to do with, and the free pizzas you sent us up didn't hurt either."

As they eat lunch, they notice another couple in the booth next to them. Kat and Emily overhear them saying, "According to Foursquare, people are saying this is a pretty good restaurant. One reviewer recommends we try the Zesty Zombie. It's got lots of meat, and we all know zombies love to eat meat." They laugh.

Kat says, "I notice that you're also doing well on the social media front."

"Yes, we copied what Miguel did at Taco Loco," Emily says. "We offered complimentary drinks, soups, salads, appetizers—you name it—to get people to write reviews for us. At first we lost a bit of money, but as you can see from the couple in the booth next to us, we dominate the reviews on Google, Foursquare, and Yelp. As a result, we get a lot of new clients to try us out."

"What about ROI and profitability as a result of this little venture?"

"Well, I can't say exactly how much more profit we've received from this, but what I can tell you is that our sales are up and some of our competitors are beginning to copy us. Some of the other restaurant owners are making gibes at Maria for stealing their customers. I know that sales are up because our SMS autoresponders are sending our regular special offers to our list without us even trying. People are coming in more frequently from these offers.

"Maria is thrilled because we have far fewer slow days. Whenever we want, we are able to craft a ridiculous offer and send it out to our database. Within an hour of sending it, we see people running through the door. All I can say is, I am not worried about my job security."

"That is so cool, Em. I am so glad you guys took the initiative and embraced SoMo Marketing so wholeheartedly. As you have said yourself, because of this strategy, other people are copying you. This makes you a market leader. Imagine if it was the other way around. Imagine if Michelangelo's Pizza did it first."

Emily shudders. "That would be horrible. We'd be playing catch-up. It takes a lot of time and planning to put these things into place. It's not as simple as just copying someone else; it's about having an intentional, premeditated market-domination strategy. Because of you and Mark, we are perceived as a market leader in Chicago. That's huge."

CHAPTER 18

NOW WHAT?

What happens next?

Well, that's up to you. You see, this story isn't really about Emily and Maria; it's about you and your business. It was written for you. How you choose to write the end to your story is completely up to you. If you've stayed with us this long, then the lessons contained within this book must have struck a chord with you. Like Maria, you know there's more you could be doing to improve your business, yet you lack something—the means, the time, the education—to make it happen. For Maria, the solution was to task an employee to do the research and make a plan. I hope we've presented you with some really good research points and an idea for a plan.

Please remember one of the greatest truths in life: if you continue to do what you've always done, you will continue to get the same results you've always gotten.

Before you stands a great opportunity to grow your business using a new social and communication phenomenon never before seen by the human race. The way people communicate has fundamentally changed. The question is, **what are *you* going to do about this?** Are you going to stand by while this change takes place around you and eventually overtakes you? Or are you going to actually take action and use this as an opportunity to innovate and grow your business? The choice is up to you.

One thing I can promise you is that if you do nothing, **someone else will** step up to the leadership position in your local area, your niche, and your area of expertise and use SoMo Marketing to rush to the top of the list.

The information contained in this book is the culmination of over twenty years of experience and research in business and marketing. You now have sufficient information to formulate a Social Mobile (SoMo) Marketing strategy for your own business.

As you read the book, you will have noticed that I talked about Mango Tree Mobile and its services. I tried to make it blend into the flow of the story to illustrate what we do and how we can help make a small business ready for SoMo Marketing. Whether you use our services or the services of another or decide to do it all yourself, I am confident that a SoMo Marketing campaign will show positive results for you. With SoMo Marketing, when you put in a bit of effort in the beginning, you receive great returns in the end—automatically. It's really an investment in your business's future.

I hope that you have found this book helpful. I ask that you honor us by forwarding a copy of this book to as many people as you can think of. Perhaps it will help their business grow, as well. As I mentioned earlier, this is a limited window of opportunity for smart businesspeople to embrace SoMo Marketing and take a leadership position in their local market, their niche, and their field.

I wish you many successes.

Please forward this book to your friends. Pay it forward.

Thank you.

Sincerely,

George Tran and the team at Mango Tree Mobile

GOT QUESTIONS?

Got questions?

Need help?

Need more information?

Are certain concepts not clear?

Do you need things explained in more detail?

I would love to hear from you and discuss your questions.

That's right! Unlike other authors, who shy away from contact, I actually want to hear what you have to say. If you have questions, then I want to hear from you.

"Why are you so open? What's the catch?" I hear you ask.

I want to hear from you because you can provide valuable feedback that will help me constantly improve the book. I'm not perfect. When people ask questions about the book, I can address them and, thus, improve the book.

One of my goals is to get this book to be a *New York Times* Best Seller. I can only do that if I make it exceptional. I hope to do that with your help. If this book hits the heights of popularity, then it has a better chance of reaching more business owners and helping more people.

Please send all your questions to support@mangotree.mobi.

About Mango Tree Mobile

Mango Tree Mobile specializes in helping small- to medium-size businesses transition their marketing and take advantage of the social-mobile marketing phenomena.

We provide clients with everything from mobile-friendly websites to social media presences, as well as SMS marketing services. Below are some of our products and services.

Mango Tree Mobile Marketing Coaching Program

While others charge thousands of dollars to create a mobile marketing strategy for you, we've created a free coaching program just for our readers. This program is created to help small business owners apply the lessons learned in this book and turn them into a real execution plan for their own business.

Unlike other education materials you find online, this program is a coaching system. We provide you with information combined with videos and an action plan in each module. Each module is then fed to you over a number of weeks in a drip-feed format. This way, you have the chance to implement what you have learned in a timely fashion without being overwhelmed by too much information all at once.

We will show you how you can create an opt-in SMS code for your business. You will learn how to create a sequential SMS auto-responder to automate your offers.

We will provide you with a copy of Emily's final checklist and organized notes so you have everything you need to implement a SoMo Marketing plan for your business.

To learn more about our absolutely free, no-strings-attached coaching program, please come to www.mangotree.mobi/coachingprogram.

Mango Sites

Is your website mobile friendly? Are all the elements designed with a mobile user in mind? Is it connected to your social media presences? If not, then we can help.

With Mango Sites, we can have your mobile-friendly website set up and ready within seven days. This includes the creation of your content, the integration with your existing social media presence, and the complete installation of your site.

The best part is that you hardly have to lift a finger. We do all the heavy lifting for you. Instead of investing hundreds of hours and an untold amount of energy getting frustrated trying to do it yourself, you can let us handle all that for you.

If you are looking for an affordable way to set up a website or convert your existing website to a mobile-friendly website, then come to MangoTreeMobile.com. We have an affordable package that includes the following:

- A front page for your business

- A "contact us" section

- An "address/hours of operation" section

- An interactive map so your visitors can find directions from their current location to your business

- Up to five photos of your business or products

- Up to five pages of content

- Links to up to five social media sites

- Installation of your mobile site

- Hosting of your mobile site

For more information about this service, come to www.mangotreemobile.com.

Mango Social

You've read about the importance of having a good social media presence online. A good social media presence could mean hundreds of free referrals for years to come for your business. However, most small businesses are woefully and inadequately equipped when it comes to this area of their business.

Do you even show up when someone does a search on Google Maps? If not, then let us put you on the map.

With Mango Social, we will help you set up a social media presence that includes:

- Setting up your Facebook fanpage for your business
- Setting up your Google Places entry
- Twitter
- Yelp
- Foursquare
- LinkedIn (if appropriate)

For more information about Mango Social, come to

www.mangotree.mobi/mangosocial.

Mango Messaging

Mango Messaging is your one-stop solution for your mobile marketing needs. When you sign up for Mango Messaging, you will have access to your own short code and be able to generate your own keywords for your mobile marketing campaigns.

You will be able to create mobile coupons, track loyalty programs, and send out sequential SMS autoresponders to your subscribers.

When you sign up, depending upon your package, you will be given a certain number of SMS credits per month to be used for your autoresponders or SMS broadcasting needs.

For more information about this service, come to www.mangotree.mobi/mangomessaging.

Mango Tree Mobile's Joint Venture Program

If you are a marketing, web design, publicity, or other similar service-providing company and would like to provide Mango Tree Mobile services to your clients as an added service in your arsenal, we have a generous JV program.

For more information about our JV program, please come to www.mangotree.mobi/jv-opportunities.

Mango Tree Mobile Certified Consultants

If you are looking for a local consultant who can give you that personal one-on-one service, then be sure to check out our certified Mango Tree Mobile consultants list. We carefully screen and review our consultants before we list them on our site.

Our certified consultants are trained in both mobile marketing and social media. They can help you implement a SoMo Marketing plan that is tailored for your business.

For more information about our Certified Mango Tree Mobile Consultants network, please come to www.mangotree.mobi/mango-marketing-consultants/.

One-on-One Consulting with George Tran

Would you like to consult with George Tran directly to formulate a personalized winning mobile strategy for your business?

If you are interested in this, please e-mail us at sales@mangotree.mobi.

Contact

You can contact us at:

Phone: 541-357-8701

E-mail: sales@mangotree.mobi

Our website is: http://www.mangotree.mobi

One-on-One Consulting with George Bunn

Consider a one-on-one consult with George Bunn that's right for you and a personalized, customized plan of action for your business.

GLOSSARY OF SOMO MARKETING TERMS

Autoresponder	Sends scheduled events to your list automatically.
Call to Action	The one step a business wants to convince the customer to take to opt in.
Lifetime Value (LTV)	How much one customer is worth to your business in dollars.
List-Acquisition Activity	An incentive program to inspire people to opt in to a business list.
List Boredom	Underselling to your list so they forget about you.
List Exhaustion	Over-solicitation of offers to a list.
List-Monetization Activity	Making offers that bring people on your list into your business to buy things.

Long Code	Uses a full phone number and keyword to opt in to an SMS list.
Loss Leader	A discounted price on a popular item that brings people in the door so they spend more on the full-priced items.
Mobile-Friendly Website	A website that is made to fit the small screens of mobile devices. It's usually simplified with only the most important information and a link to the desktop website. Because it is a more basic version, it loads quickly and is easily navigated.
Mobile Marketing	The act of attracting customers and business using mobile phones and devices.
Mobile Strategy	A marketing plan that incorporates Mobile Marketing.
Opt-In List	A list of people acquired by a business when people provide their contact information to allow that business to market to them.
QR Code	Square bar codes that are scanned into mobile devices to bring business information to customers.
ROI (Return On Investment)	A mathematical ratio of money gained or lost on an investment (i.e., a marketing investment like a radio advertisement) relative to the amount of money originally invested.
Short Code	A short SMS text number combined with a keyword used to opt-in to a list.

SMS	Simple messaging system, commonly referred to as a text message.
Social Media	Where people gather online to discuss and communicate. Examples are Facebook, Twitter, Yelp, LiveJournal, and so many more.
SoMo Marketing	Social and Mobile Marketing for businesses.

If you continue to do what you've always done, you will continue to get the same results you've always gotten.

Take Charge of Your Business.

Take Massive Action Today.